Coleman

ALTERNATIVES
to
DESPAIR

To my children, Howard, Julie, and Hope, whose presence in my life helps keep me working for a better world.

ALTERNATIVES
to
DESPAIR

Leon H. Sullivan

Judson Press, Valley Forge

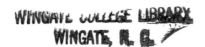

Library of Congress Cataloging in Publication Data

Sullivan, Leon Howard, 1922-
    Alternatives to despair, Valley Forge, Judson Press,
1972.
    Includes bibliographical references.
    1. Negroes—Economic conditions. 2. Opportunities Industrialization Center, Philadelphia. 3. Negroes—Religion. I. Title.
E185.8.S92   301.45'19'6073   72-432
ISBN 0-8170-0570-6

Printed in the U.S.A.

WHAT KIND
OF BOOK
IS THIS?

I have done a lot of speaking and writing in the past ten or fifteen years about the things I believe in. Many others have added their records through both the oral and printed word. Many times I am tempted to think that there have been too many words. Let the deeds speak for themselves.

But then I have second thoughts about it all. Interpretation is needed. If the things I have tried to do for the advancement of the Black man socially and economically are charged off to motivations such as group self-interest, do-goodism, or responsible citizenship, then my interpreters have missed the main point. My story, at least up to a few years ago, has been told in another book entitled *Build Brother Build*. My theology has been preached each Sunday in Philadelphia's Zion Baptist Church. But I do not feel that I have succeeded in articulating the connection between my economic programs and my theology effectively enough up to this time.

In this book, therefore, I want to explain the underlying theological basis that has motivated a Black preacher to

55476

spend major parts of his time and energy in business matters closely related to the social and economic development of his people. I believe this is what any Christian who is worth his salt must do. He must have a secure faith that he can declare when the occasion calls for it, and he must practice this faith through his involvement in the day-to-day activities and concerns to which the unfolding pathway of his life leads him.

In this book, then, I am concerned with the why and wherefore of my actions and beliefs. Each of the four basic chapters tells a little about some important phase of my work but a great deal more about the reasons for it. Each chapter is then followed by a group of sermons and addresses, which I have delivered at Zion or in other settings, directly related to the concerns of that chapter.

I don't claim to be either a great businessman or a great preacher. If you pressed me, I could name many men who would excel me in either field. But I do try very hard to practice what I preach and to preach what I practice. If in any way this book helps you to go through the same mental process that it has forced upon me—to relate your personal theology to your actions toward your fellowman—then I will feel that it has been worth the effort.

LEON H. SULLIVAN

I SEE FREEDOM

Now I have a promise of the future.
Hope on the now-seen nearing shore comes clear.
I see Freedom! And I can live in pride,
Walking into new tomorrows.
                                   —Leon H. Sullivan

CONTENTS

1
WHAT
ATTITUDE
CAN DO

As far back as I can recall from my childhood, I've believed that something could be done to assist the plight of the Black man in America—in fact, to help the needs of the poor and underprivileged generally. As a boy born in the hill country of West Virginia I knew poverty firsthand. I knew what it was because I experienced it, because I saw people all about me living in need. This problem was my great concern.

As I grew up, I thought of various possible ways of dealing with race and poverty. I knew that a man was neither inferior because he was Black nor superior because he was White. I was convinced that a man is a man. In my opinion the opportunities and conditions in which he must live determine what he can become.

My earliest days in Charleston, the capital of West Virginia, made me realize that the solutions were eventually to come which would help my people. In this context I became aware that the basic core for these solutions would have to come from God. I believed this although as a youth most of the churches I attended did not deal directly with social issues. Their services were filled with emotions and the preaching was highly excitable.

The message of the preaching and the lessons from the Bible over and over said to me, "God can lift a man if a man will let God lift him." Through high school and then through college I held to this point of view until finally I received God's call to become a minister.

There were many factors which led to my becoming a minister. Perhaps the most important was the influence, the inspiration of a saintly grandmother who more than anyone else had to do with my upbringing and my religious orientation. Although she was perhaps unable to read or write, she constantly kept before me the importance of God in my life and urged upon me the importance of service to God in my future days. Another spiritual influence upon me was a young minister by the name of the Reverend Moses Newsome who came to the big Black church in Charleston, the First Baptist Church. His example when I was at a highly impressionable age influenced me toward the Christian ministry. His spiritual leadership was characterized by a commitment to help the downtrodden. He taught me that Christ's message to the homefolk in Nazareth permeated our Lord's every deed.

> "The Spirit of the Lord is upon me,
> because he has anointed me to preach good news to the poor.
> He has sent me to proclaim release to the captives
> and recovering of sight to the blind,
> to set at liberty those who are oppressed,
> to proclaim the acceptable year of the Lord."
>
> —Luke 4:18-19

The particular key to the future of the Black man, as I saw it, was assistance to the needs of the poor and underprivileged. This was and is the message that must not only be articulated in sermons but also be exemplified in deeds: To me the church had to be more than a voice; the church had to be a demonstration of the will of God for men on earth.

13

Ministry must be geared to action. To me the gospel could not be valid if it merely dealt with irrelevant discussions such as how many angels could dance upon the point of a needle. To me this kind of thing could not help man; it could bring no hope of salvation to a child whose stomach was empty, whose feet were bare, whose body was naked! If the gospel of Jesus Christ was to be really meaningful, it had to prove itself through what it did to help men live on earth. Heaven was coming, but until that day the pearly gates could take care of themselves.

This conviction, this belief, that the basic solution to the problems of our society must come somehow by the efforts of the church and the churchmen, was a burning belief within me. The experience of becoming deeply concerned about the problems that I saw in the back hills of West Virginia where there was so much deprivation and need was not an isolated incident. I later saw these conditions over and over again as I experienced other sections of America—the Black Belt, the Delta, Appalachia, and the concentrated cities of America. I became frightfully aware that the solutions could not be found alone in the political government or among secular leaders. Politicians and social workers could take significant practical actions to assist the underprivileged and the poor to ameliorate some of the conditions that abounded. But the real surge, the direction, the course to be taken, in my opinion, had to come through the church as God's agent working toward the ultimate development of solutions that could truly deal with the conditions.

I saw my special mission in the Christian ministry as the proclamation of the gospel which tells me that God loves and helps the underprivileged. I have remained in that mold and have not found it necessary to change. I feel that in this way the church is being relevant to the needs of the times.

I shout on Sunday that there are not enough day-by-day Christians who strive to work out the soul salvation of the community. There are not enough Christians dealing with the problems where people are, the gut problems, the problems of the high and the mighty—the problems which the middle-class man cannot find time or does not wish to find time to solve! Is it because he considers them too unimportant? Or is it because the challenges are too time-consuming or because he is afraid to deal with the distressed, the militant, the disadvantaged, and the mentally retarded? He is like the man walking on the other side of the street refusing to lend a hand to the man in the hole because he is too busy hurrying on to the temple for worship and prayer.

I saw the need for the Samaritan of our time who would stop and reach down and take off his own clothes, if necessary, to wrap the wounds of a bleeding brother. I was challenged to participate in a ministry that was not only of the pulpit, but was of the streets, an enacting, living, lifting, pulsating, saving ministry. This was not to be a political movement but a religious community, pragmatically dealing with the needs of men on earth while it also tended to the needs of their souls. I was convinced that a man's body and soul could not be separated. (As the body physically disintegrates in life and yet is renewed and retained, so the soul continues to exist and even to be renewed.) The ultimates of eternity are intertwined with man's physical person and his spiritual person. They are indeed one with time.

When I moved from West Virginia to New York City and labored in Harlem with the problems of youth, crime, and drugs, I was unconsciously training myself for the main effort. All of my experiences in Harlem affected what the future of my work would be. It was as though I were in school, engaged in some training program of which I was not aware which was preparing me for what God wanted me to do. God has a way of preparing us for the work we are to do in spite of ourselves. In Harlem my work in the community was largely through community groups, such as the March-on-Washington movement, led by one of the greatest Black Americans of the century, A. Phillip Randolph, under whose tutelage I learned the basic ideas of nonviolent direct action and the development of community power through effective community organizations.

My experiences as assistant minister at the Abyssinian Church, pastored by the dynamic and highly articulate late Adam Clayton Powell, also had a major influence on my determination to relate the role of the church to the community. Adam Powell was an effective teacher in community organization as well as in political education.

Leaving the glamour of Harlem after getting married to a sensible young lady, I was helped by my new young wife to understand that my feet were riding off the ground like a balloon. If I did not get back down to earth, a little pinprick would explode the balloon and there would be nothing left of me. We therefore left New York for New Jersey, where I became pastor of a wonderful little church, First Baptist, in the small community of South Orange. There for five years I continued my formal education while experimenting in church-related community development projects.

One of the big problems facing any young minister is that his theology is likely to be too narrow for the broad kind of work that he is going to have to do. All theological training should be concerned with community-related programs in a day such as this. What happens to the people of the community is as important to theological expression as is a sermon on Sunday morning. We pastors too often don't realize that three-quarters of the people who listen to our religious discourses don't know anything about what we're talking about when it comes to theology—and very often even we ourselves don't understand what we are talking about.

For this day the minister must be geared and trained not just in "Thus saith the Lord" but in "What saith the Lord to help the people, and how do we get it done?" Otherwise our ministry is like a stool with one leg; it will not hold up; it is bound to keel over. In this respect the whole spectrum of theological education is going to have to undergo a complete

new process of development and organization. Attention needs to be given to the community responsibilities of the church in terms of such matters as community education and political determination, as well as the concept of the Christian way and the books of the Bible. The prophet of old acted in concrete situations. He combined theology and action. He was really a statesman, in the sense of Demosthenes,

> to discern events in their beginnings, to be beforehand in the detection of movements and tendencies, and to forewarn his countrymen accordingly; to fight against the political vices, from which no state is free, of procrastination, supineness, ignorance, and party jealousy; to impress upon all the paramount importance of unity and friendly feeling, and the duty of providing promptly for the country's needs.[1]

[1] John Paterson, *The Goodly Fellowship of the Prophets* (New York: Charles Scribner's Sons, 1950), pp. 79-80.

17

Not so important as what *was* done is what *can be* done. Every minister, every young person who is taking any kind of theological education, should spend at least a year in practical field work, not just a few hours, but a long span of time, totally involved as an intern in community-related church work. It is imperative that we have persons in the ministry who have learned how to deal with dope addicts and to struggle for the full implementation of civil rights laws. They need to be able to coach community baseball teams, to serve as educational assistants to vocational printing programs, and as prison teachers—or even to work in OIC, which is our major project.

After five years of preparation in South Orange, I was called to Philadelphia's Zion Baptist Church, and I believed it was time to move on. In Philadelphia I could put my philosophies to work within a great problem-filled urban area. Having worked with young people in community organizations in New York and New Jersey, I was now led to the creation of OIC, the Opportunities Industrialization Center. This spin-off of the civil rights movement was designed to help Blacks, Spanish-speaking, and other minority Americans receive skills for jobs that were becoming massively available.

Let us look at the background of OIC. Prior to its development four hundred Black preachers in Philadelphia had organized selective patronage programs. These were planned strategies of dealing with one company at a time, withholding Black consumer patronage until jobs in that firm were made available to Blacks and other minorities who had previously been discriminated against in job opportunities. I had developed a plan to carry on this selective action program and had devoted three solid years with many of my brother ministers to its implementation. A highly selective patronage program was perhaps the most significant community tool used in urban centers to open up desirable industrial jobs and good business opportunities to Blacks. In Philadelphia one-half million Blacks have cooperated in the program during its existence and thousands of new job situations have been opened to our people.

Because our people up to this time had been excluded from the jobs that were now becoming available, however, many did not have the necessary skills to qualify for the newly opened employment opportunities. Blacks in the past had concluded that there was no need to train for these jobs, because they were not available to Blacks anyway. Because Black people could not reasonably expect even to be considered for blue-collar-middle-income jobs, 95 percent of them worked in what we call service occupations.

As we began to break segregation and to solve the problems of integration through the selective patronage program, employment opportunities in Philadelphia increased and the call came forth for Black workers to fill the jobs that were newly available. But now we found that our people were not prepared for these new job opportunities. Furthermore, industry was not interested in preparing Blacks for these jobs; in fact, most firms were only looking for excuses not to hire them, saying, "We told you so! We offered you the jobs and you can't do them." I found that integration without preparation is frustration, and that the needed massive efforts toward this preparation would have to be made in the Black community itself. The Black community would have to do the job that had to be done realizing that the White man, the White industrial leader, still was not going to do it for us. And I for one didn't want to take any bets that he would really help us even if he said he would.

Looking at the magnitude of the problem with the ever-increasing congestion of Blacks in the large cities such as Philadelphia, I realized that programs had to be designed not just for a month or a season but for a long period of time. Ultimately not hundreds, but thousands and tens of thousands, of people had to be reached with new kinds of training and new training mechanisms.

Thus, the first Opportunities Industrialization Center, and

19

with it the OIC movement, was born in an old jailhouse that had been standing empty for four years with a basement half filled with water, which had no finished walls, no windows, no lights—just bare cells standing there as evidence of what used to be a jailhouse, the main center of agony and frustration and despair in the Philadelphia Black community. I determined that we could change that jail from a place of despair to a place of hope. And transforming that building would be the symbol that we could begin to transform human beings and human lives even as Christ said that men could be born again. We were convinced that we could translate the gospel in a new way—a pragmatic way, a productive way —to show that God does have power in his hands to change the lives of men to give them hope. Although the gospel wasn't preached in terms of the sermon at OIC, it was preached in the formulation of the program and the development of the concept and in its slogan: *"Self Help*—We help ourselves."

This program was destined to prove that what matters most is not where a man comes from, but where with the help of God he is going. OIC is, as much as anything I know, a translation of the gospel of Jesus Christ into pragmatic terms, for every individual who comes to OIC comes not only as an individual but as a soul to be lifted and to be helped. But, even if a man is able to stand on his own two feet, the sense of belief in himself and the capacity and ability to earn his own way and to make a life for himself and his family will help his soul increase. This confidence will help his soul to be in a position to be free to receive the preaching of the gospel. Then he can take over and do the rest. I know that no man can accept God and love him throughout life, on an empty stomach. Nor can he worship when he sees his children living in a black hole which they can't get out of because nobody seems to be doing anything or to care.

The OIC program deals principally with two factors, a man's attitude and his skill. This program made such an impact on the community that in time results of the work began to show in every neighborhood of the Philadelphia community. Twelve thousand or more people have been trained and placed on jobs in Philadelphia as a result of the centers that are very active in every part of the city. Fifteen hundred men and women were trained at a time, while thousands and thousands more were on the waiting list.

Typical of the kind of training courses OIC has already offered are these:

Merchandising-Marketing
IBM Key Punch Operation
Electronics Technician
Computer Maintenance
Secretarial Skills
Office Machine Practice
Communications Skills
Computational Skills
Printing and Graphic Arts
Commercial Cooking
Restaurant Practices
Clerk Typing
Commercial Art
Office Machine Repair
Bowling Machine Repair
Laundry and Dry Cleaning
Power Sewing
Plumbing
Air-Conditioning and Refrigeration
Brick Masonry
Electricity
Chemistry Laboratory Technician
Sheet Metal
Teletype
Machine Tool Operation

Electronics Assembly
Drafting
Welding

The instructional program is geared to individual differences. Trainees are taken from where they come into the program and moved progressively onward until they are job-ready. This is all done by instructors who gear each lesson to the needs of each trainee. Each person gets an opportunity to exhibit his skill, dexterity, or self-reliance.

Included as a critical part of all OIC training functions is the special preparation called the *Feeder Program*. Each person who enters the OIC training program is required to enroll first in this attitudinal motivational program. This prevocational training provides the foundation necessary for many trainees to (1) accept the idea of going to school, (2) understand basic communicative and computational skills, and (3) be motivated to a point where a more than reasonable certainty can be established that he will remain on a job once trained and placed.

After this prevocational training, the trainees are "fed" into the vocational training courses of their selection. From this action comes the "Feeder Program" name. It is here where OIC differs sharply from other manpower-training programs. Its flexibility and its Feeder Program are considered by many to be the two prime reasons why OIC is the great success it is. In fact, OIC's Feeder Program concept could be of considerable value to other job-training programs.

Once a potential trainee registers, he is assigned to a counselor. There his interests and desires are determined and recorded. Personal problems are discussed and steps taken to help eliminate them. The counselor becomes the trainee's closest associate at OIC. A very personal relationship is established, and, more often than not, the encouragement and assistance necessary to keep a trainee moving ahead come in private conferences between trainee and counselor. This

counselor-trainee relationship follows as long as the trainee is associated with OIC.

Some trainees complete the Feeder Program and go directly to jobs under on-the-job training contracts with industry. Others go into vocational training courses. There is no "beginning" and "completion" in the feeder classes. When a trainee is enrolled, the teacher fits him in, starting him at his level of achievement. He remains there until he receives a favorable nod from the counselor-teacher team to move ahead. This individual touch, this personal concern is what keeps OIC out in front in the eyes of the very people who are being trained.

OIC's operations constitute new approaches in providing supportive services as an integral part of an overall training and motivational program. OIC is indeed a new institution. It has demonstrated that a coordinated program providing comprehensive services can effectively deal with the manifold problems of poor, unmotivated, and educationally deficient adults. All training is, of course, carefully structured by a combination of experienced OIC training people and members of local Industrial Advisory Councils, who are fully informed on current and future employment needs. All OIC faculty members are experienced instructors, each of them having an excellent familiarity with industry's requirements.

Having succeeded in securing federal funds for OIC, the community is continuing to respond in support of the program. Contributions amounting to hundreds of thousands of dollars have also come from individuals, industrial organizations, companies, religious groups, and church organizations. OIC became a household word in Philadelphia. In fact, former U.S. President Lyndon Johnson, who paid a surprise visit to OIC during his last year in the White House, declared that OIC was the most successful poverty program active in the nation.

From Philadelphia the OIC program began to multiply.

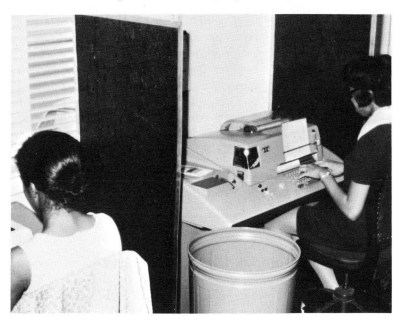

Centers appeared in more than one hundred cities across the nation, becoming the first massive industrial manpower training movement ever initiated in the country's history. The movement was created by a Black man with the assistance of Black leaders such as my dear friend, the Reverend Thomas Ritter, a remarkable individual who became the first executive director of Philadelphia's OIC. The total group in its founding believed in God and held that this was a work of God in the community and for the world.

The Power of Believing
A SERMON

"I can do all things in him who strengthens me."
—Philippians 4:13

One of the most powerful forces in all the world is the power of thought, for what a man thinks makes that man what he is and what he will be. If there is anything that makes a man akin to God, it is his power to think, to believe, to rationalize, to make decisions about himself, about others, and about things. If a man, for example, believes that a straight line is the shortest distance between two points, then for him this is true, in spite of the fact that there is no such thing as a really straight line in a crooked world. Or if a man believes that a rabbit's foot in his pocket will give him good luck, then for him this is true, in spite of the fact that the rabbit had four of them and it didn't help him at all. If a man believes that a black cat crossing his path will give him bad luck, then for him this will be true, because a man will always find what he is looking for if it is in his mind. What a man thinks makes him what he is—or makes things happen to him in his life.

Nowadays we are all concerned about old age, so that when a person becomes sixty-five years of age or more, he often thinks that he has one foot in the grave, and the other on a banana peel. But, if a man or a woman believes that chronological age is not the measure as much as spiritual and psychological age, it is amazing what this outlook will do for the longevity of his years. Even now there is intensive consideration in Washington to re-evaluate, to reanalyze, and possibly to revamp our whole system of retirement, because we have learned that some of the most dynamic and creative thinking going on in the nation today is among people who are between the years of fifty-nine and seventy-four. If an individual *believes* that he is old, then he *is* old, and if he *believes* that his time is measured, then it *is* measured. When he becomes sixty-five, if he believes he is about to die, then he is already dead.

This principle holds true also in matters of health and illness. Physicians have concluded that much of the illness in America today is illness in the mind more than in the body, for many things that we think have happened to us physiologically are really things that have been created in our minds, in our own thoughts. A boy once went to a movie with his girl friend and in the middle of the movie she elbowed him and complained that she had a terrible headache. He acted as though he didn't hear her because it was right in the middle of the movie when the hero and the girl were getting together and he wanted to see what was going to happen. She elbowed him again and said, "I have a terrible headache." Then quickly he thought and he put something in her hand and said, "Now, you put this under your tongue and in a little while you will feel much better." She put it under her tongue and a few seconds later she said, "I feel fine." When the movie was over and they were walking under the marquee, she looked up at him and said, "What kind of pill was that you gave me for the headache? It was the best I have ever taken." He said, "Take it from under your tongue and look at it." She did and it was a button from his shirt.

Many illnesses that plague us really have their seats in our minds. This is true even of cancer. Psychiatrists who are involved in medical psychiatry say that more and more it is becoming clear that a major reason for the development of cancerous growth in the individual can be psychological. Of course, there are physical reasons, too, but the psychological factors cannot be ignored.

So with life. The power of believing in one's capability and in the power of God in an individual's life helps him to grow, especially spiritually in this world. The entire philosophy of Jesus

Christ was built around the power of faith and belief. Over and over again he inspired individuals to believe in themselves and in what they could do. Jesus infused the man who was lame with a new power of faith in his own capability to rise and take up his bed and walk. The fishermen who were washing their nets along the Lake of Gennesaret were inspired to fish again, because Jesus infused Peter with the power of faith and belief that he could do what seemed impossible. And on and on throughout the Bible and the experiences of Jesus, we find in his sermons, his philosophy, and his life characteristics of the power of believing in what God can do with a man or a woman once that person finds faith in him.

I am acquainted with a wonderful man who was born some forty years ago on the east side of New York. He was born with no legs. He was reared in a cold-water flat in a divided home, poor. As he went out pushing himself on a wagon improvised with wheels, children laughed at him. Adults walked by—many of them—and with great sorrow looked upon him with compassion that struck the seat of his mind. Somehow he grew up believing that God would give him legs of the spirit. His mother would pick him up on Sundays and take him to Mass where he could hear the intonations of the priest and where he could be infused with the power of faith from God, believing that God somehow could help him to walk, even if he didn't have legs.

The young man is now the head of an enterprise on Long Island, New York, that employs more than four hundred men and women who are incapacitated—people with no arms, no legs, or no eyes— in meaningful employment. He is the administrator of an enterprise that in past years has grossed millions and millions of dollars. He is the conveyor of a whole new spirit within the world of those who have handicaps, helping them to know that if they believe in God, God will help them to make useful meanings of their lives. His name is Henry Viscardi, Jr., of Abilities Enterprise. He says, "I believe God is able." Here is a man who learned to believe in God in spite of previous conditions of circumstance.

This is the heart of the gospel of Jesus. If an individual can believe in God, he can stand on legs even if he doesn't have them, for God will give him legs of the spirit to walk on. We must learn to believe in God and in the power that God can give to all of us to cleanse our cities of sin and evil and bigotry, which are the real causes of violence, disorder, and anger in our streets. The problem facing the American population is not the problem of so-called violence of Black men, nor the reactions of Whites against Blacks, but the problem of sin—Whites being unchristian in their actions and attitudes toward Blacks—the problem of sin and prejudice and bigotry.

This question of how we think and how we act toward our brother affects not only what happens in race relations but also what happens in our homes, in our neighborhoods, and in our churches. Let us believe in the Word of God and the power of God to change things in our cities, but first to change things in our own minds and our own thoughts. Let us hope and pray that reasons which have brought us together here will open up our minds and our hearts to the revelation of a great God who is the author of positive thinking and positive action of man toward his fellowman. May this service lift us in our minds, in our hearts, and in our thoughts so that each of us might get closer to God—realizing that to the extent we do get closer to God, so will God strengthen us and be closer to us. Let us remember, most of all, in proportion as we get closer to God, we also get closer to each other, and take hands equally as brothers of our fellowmen, children of one family, fathered by one great God of all.

This is the power of belief: Believe in yourself, believe in your life, believe in what you can do; and God will give you power that you never thought you had before, prolong your years, and make you more useful in this world in which we live.

Let us pray:

Now, great God, give us thy power to believe in ourselves, and in what we do, and in what we can be, and in what we are. May the grace of Jesus Christ be with us all.
Amen.

The Little Red Hen

A SERMON

"Then he said to his disciples, 'The harvest is plentiful, but the laborers are few; pray therefore the Lord of the harvest to send out laborers into his harvest.'"   —*Matthew 9:37-38*

Whatever you get that is worthwhile in life has to be worked for. Nothing of value comes easily. Anything standing that is secure has taken effort and work on the part of someone to make it a reality. Unfortunately there are so many who think they can get something for nothing; but the world just isn't made like that. Whatever a person gets of substance and value in life requires a lot of effort.

If you want a good neighborhood to live in, you have to work at it. Those of us who live in Black communities, where the services are often poor, have to work at making our neighborhoods look like something. To keep our streets clean, we have to work at it. To keep garbage and trash off the sidewalks, we have to work at it. To keep taprooms out of our neighborhoods, we have to work at it. To keep the street quiet, we have to work at it. To keep gangs from forming and taking over where we live, we have to get together and work at it. To keep things clean and attractive where we live, we have to sweep and wash to keep it so. We can't depend on someone else to do it for us. Usually City Hall and the suburbs don't care. We have to do it for ourselves.

If you want a good home life, you have to work at it. Good marriages don't fall out of the sky, and good marriages aren't necessarily made in heaven. A man and woman have to work at making a marriage good down here on earth. As years go by, a marriage should get mellower and mellower, "Sweeter as the days go by." But if the husband and wife don't work at it (and mind you I said *husband and wife,* for a good home requires the cooperation of both), however much love there was when the marriage started, the home won't last. And when I say home, I don't mean the house or the furniture or the rugs, but a place where people live in peace and understanding and respect for each other.

If you want your children to be raised properly, you have to work at it. According to an old saying, "As the twig is bent, so grows the tree." A child has to be raised and not just allowed to grow. In today's world, instead of children being raised by their parents, too many children are raising their parents. And instead of the parents telling the child what to do, children are telling their parents what to do. The Bible tells us: "Train up a child in the way he should go, and when he is old he will not depart from it" (Proverbs 22:6). Raising children requires work —hard work and time and sacrifice and prayer—and day-by-day effort. Bringing a child up "in the way he should go" should start from the cradle and continue through the early years, until the child is able to stand on his own feet and makes his own way.

We have given youth too much freedom in some wrong directions. We let our children do anything they want to do. Bereft of guidance and direction they just "go." But you can't put an adult's head on a child's body. As a child grows, someone has to tell him right from wrong. A child doesn't know himself. To raise our children properly, we have to work at it.

By the same principles, if we want the church to prosper, we can't just come to church and sit down on Sunday mornings and hope everything will turn out all right in the community and in the world. Far more is required than that. We have to do more than just "sit down." Part of our present problem is that we have been sitting down on God too long. It is time we started "getting up" and going out into the highways and byways and letting men and women know that Jesus lives. The Bible is right when it says: "The harvest is plentiful, but the laborers are few" (Matthew 9:37). The church needs more workers with *faith* enough and *spirit* enough and *religion* enough to go out into the streets where the needs of men and women are greatest, to tell men and women and boys and girls "Jesus lives!" and to tell them "Jesus saves!" and to tell them "Jesus lifts!" and "Jesus cleanses!" and that a man has a soul to be saved and a God to glorify!

There is no magic formula for getting things done. There is no hocus-pocus about success. To be successful in anything, personal or impersonal, a person has to work at it. It is hard for some of us to understand this philosophy of working to get things done, but we had better begin to understand it.

The fundamental need for any race today is the need to work for progress. And the fundamental need for the church today is to work for salvation. There is a slogan that goes: "Work always wins." And as far as I know, this is pretty true everywhere. So let's not sit around and wait for things to come our way—or for someone to do things for us that we can do for ourselves. *Rather,* trust in God, hold to God's hand, and work and pray and "Help yourself." And in time, those who have stood by on the side-lines, making excuses and doing other things while you were doing what had to be done, will see the value of what you have done.

There is no better illustration of what I am saying than that little children's story called "The Little Red Hen." Let me tell you about it. This little nursery tale tells of five animals who lived on a farm together. One was a little dog who was always barking and busy running around in the other fellow's yard and getting into trouble. One was a little cat who spent most of his time hiding in a corner, sleeping his life away, when he was not chasing after the birds. One was a little pig who could always be found wallowing in mud puddles. One was a little duck who could always be seen switching and strutting around. And one was Little Red Hen, who was always busy, working hard, scratching the ground for food.

One day, Little Red Hen found some wheat seeds. She asked her little friends to help her plant the seeds, but all of them were too busy to help. The dog was running, the cat was sleeping, the pig was wallowing, the duck was switching, and none of them had time to give. So Little Red Hen went on and planted the seeds herself. When the seeds grew into wheat, Little Red Hen needed someone to help her cut down the wheat. Once again she asked her friends to give her a hand. Unfortunately, though, they were all still too busy to help. So Little Red Hen went on and cut down the wheat herself. When the wheat was cut, Little Red Hen needed someone to help her carry the wheat to the mill to be ground into flour. Again she asked her friends for help, but they were still too busy. The dog was running, the cat sleeping, the pig wallowing and grunting, and the duck still strutting and switching herself about.

So—Little Red Hen took the wheat to the mill herself, and it was ground into flour. Then Little Red Hen came back home and made the flour into cookies. While the cookies were baking, the delicious aroma spread all over the farm. They smelled so good. When the cookies were done and ready for eating, Little Red Hen called out to her friends, "Who will help me eat the cookies?" And, all of a sudden, everything changed.

"I will," said the dog (who, all of a sudden had no place to go), standing up on his two hind legs with his tongue sticking out, panting, ready for some cookies.

"I will," said the cat (who, all of a sudden had become very much awake), with eyes wide open and two paws sticking out.

"I will," said the pig, who came over and sat down and somehow had a napkin tied around his neck.

"I will," said the duck, who had stopped switching and strutting long enough to call out. Everyone was ready to eat when the cookies were finished.

But Little Red Hen said: "I found the seed myself, I planted the seed myself, I cut down the wheat myself, and I carried the wheat to the mill myself. So, I'll just eat the cookies myself." And she did.

Now, what Little Red Hen did may not seem Christian. Doesn't Christianity teach that we should share what we have? But Little Red Hen could have been following the old Chinese proverb: "No work—no eat." So in life: No work—no eat. You will be lucky to get crumbs from the table. You get, for the most part, what you work for. And, if my memory serves me correctly, that's just about what Jesus was teaching in the parable of the talents.

Now, that is the story of the Little Red Hen. Let us look deeper into it, and particularly into the characteristics of the little animals on the farm, because I am sure their characteristics will remind you of people you know.

First, there was the little dog, who spent most of his time running around in someone else's yard. There was work to do at home, but that didn't interest him. His sights were set somewhere else. The little dog had his priorities in another direction. Instead of doing what needed to be done at home, he was busy running off someplace else. Instead of minding his own business, he spent his time getting in other people's business.

Now, don't you know people like that? They can find time for everything else they want to do, except what they ought to do. They are experts on advice to everyone else, but they don't have time to take care of the "home front." They can tell the other fellow how to take care of his business, but they don't take care of their own business. They forget the "home front."

This is one of the big things wrong with America today. We can tell the world what to do, but we don't take care of the "home front." We tell the world that democracy is the answer to the world's ills, but we don't practice democracy on the home front. So the rest of the world says to America: "I hear what you say, but why don't you practice what you preach?" The world is saying to America: "Before you tell us what to do, take care of your 'home front.'"

And as Christians, we have to make our religion a reality at home. You can talk all you want to about Jesus and Christianity and the Bible; and you can sing, and you can pray, and you can shout; but if you don't practice your religion in your life, something is wrong with your religion.

We of the church have to get ourselves straightened out first. Charity begins at home and spreads abroad. As Christians we must get our own houses in order; then the world will listen. "Get the beam out of your own eye." "Physician, heal yourself."

Then, there was the little cat—always in a corner taking a nap —the lazy cat, too tired to do much worthwhile, sleeping the time away. Oh, my friends, so many of us are like that, sleeping life away. While others, like Little Red Hen, are working, we are busy sleeping.

I fear this is one sad characteristic of our race. We sleep too much. Now I know sleeping is a form of escape; and we do have a lot to want to escape from. But sleeping isn't going to make problems we face go away. Rather, with our problems we have to stay awake *more,* so we will have more time to work on the problems. As a race we sleep too much, literally and figuratively. Educationally we are asleep; economically we are asleep. Politically we are asleep. We have to wake up. And when we do, we shall see real progress made.

And in the church we have been asleep. In fact, so much so that the Communists call our religion "the opiate of the people."

In our churches things are dark and dismal, and dreary and gloomy. No wonder so many of us go to sleep in church. The atmosphere puts people to sleep. Even the hymns we sing are a hundred years old. But this is not what the church ought to be like. The church of God is intended to be bright and light and happy and joyful. "Make a joyful noise to the Lord, all the lands!" (Psalm 100:1). "I am the light of the world," said Jesus (John 8:12). "I came that they may have life, and have it abundantly," he said (John 10:10). Jesus wants us to wake up in the church—and to stop being so dead! Anything that is dead ought to be buried, and much that goes on in the churches ought to be buried.

We must wake up and live and get busy helping the Little Red Hens who are working to build a better city and a better world and a more relevant and vibrant church. If we would wake up, we would find that the church has great power and Christians have great power. God has all power in his hands, and he lets us use it. But we have to get up and get busy working for the Lord to see that power realized. Twelve men changed the world, and a church like ours could change this whole city if we started living our religion. Christians must wake up. Jesus said: "We must work the works of him who sent me, while it is day; night comes, when no man can work" (John 9:4).

Then there was the little pig, satisfied, wallowing in mud and garbage and filth. He wasn't willing to help Little Red Hen; in fact, he wasn't even interested in helping himself. To help others, you must want to help yourself. No person has to live in filth if he doesn't want to live there. If a person has the desire to improve the way he lives, he can. No one has to wallow in filth. It does not matter how low a person falls in life; if a person has the will to get up and is willing to let Jesus help him, he can get up.

Ask God to keep you out of the mudholes, because mudholes are all around us. And if you don't watch where you are going, you are prone to fall into one. So ask God to guide you around the mudholes. Ask God to keep you clean—mentally clean, morally clean, spiritually clean. Ask God to give you clean hands, minds, bodies, and hearts to work for Jesus Christ.

Then there was the little duck. She couldn't help Little Red

Hen because she was too busy showing off. She spent her time strutting and switching around, looking cute. Now I like to see ladies look beautiful. God doesn't want you to look ugly—God wants you to look good; and if you serve God, you will look good. But the problem here was that the little duck was more interested in how she was looking than in what she was doing. "Beauty is as beauty does." The little duck concentrated on how she looked: her pretty feathers, her pretty feet, her pretty walk, and her pretty talk. She had beauty on the outside, but she didn't have the right spirit on the inside. So it didn't matter how she looked on the outside.

Let us strive to get the beauty of Christ on the inside, and real beauty will be revealed on the outside. If we have religion on the inside, it will show up in how we look and in what we do on the outside. The duck didn't help, because she was more interested in how she looked than in what needed to be done.

But Little Red Hen didn't let any of this stop her—not the busy dog, the lazy cat, the wallowing pig, or the show-off duck. Little Red Hen had a job to do. And she just went on doing her job. And when she had finished planting and cutting and carrying and cooking, she ended with the cookies.

My friends, work does win! As a nation and as a church and as individuals, work does win. The world is looking at us. Let us live so the world can see beauty in our lives.

And in serving Christ, working while it is still day, let us strive to live and work for the Lord until one day we hear that welcome voice saying:

"Well done, good and faithful servant; you have been faithful over a little, I will set you over much" (Matthew 25:21).

The Spiritual Interpretation of Freedom Through the Christian Experience of Frederick Douglass

A SERMON

It is to the Black community, and specifically to the rejectors and skeptics of the Black church, that this sermon is directed. I am speaking to those who, through education and exposure to Western culture, have outgrown the religion of their ancestors; who cannot tolerate emotionalism; who cannot communicate with God from that noisy arena of the ignorant masses; and to those who know so much that they believe neither the preacher nor the Bible nor the church has anything to say to them.

My sermon is also directed to those whose concept of God is so limited they can only envision him as White, and therefore avoid him, not knowing that God is colorless and is a Spirit; and to those who reject the Black church because they believe it is filled with Uncle Toms and has made little contribution to the advancement of the race.

And most of all, this sermon is directed to those *who do not believe in God* because they think he is either the grand fooler of the universe or a casualty of the generation gap who has been retired and replaced by Sigmund Freud with his sex psychology.

I will attempt to demonstrate the authenticity of the religion experienced by Blacks on this soil, as it evolved from slavery, a slavery which was more devastating than that experienced by the Jews in Egypt.

I want to call your attention, not to the theories of sociologists, but to the words and example of Frederick Douglass, who one day was told by God that he had work to do—and to the music, poetry, prose, and experiences of the Black people themselves, as the Bible and their church and their God spoke to them in the midst of their bondage.

Before I go further, I want to define religion briefly. To do this, it will be necessary to discuss what religion appears to be, what it is, and what it is not. One thing is sure, religion is not what many think—a lot of precious talk. An old admonition says, "Pay less attention to what a child says, and more attention to what he does." A child cannot only fool you; he can fool himself. And religion as we know it has the same capability. It can make you fool yourself! So religion is not words but works. Jesus said: "Even though you do not believe me, believe the works, that you may know and understand that the Father is in me and I am in the Father" (John 10:38).

Real religion is the channel through which man can achieve a harmonious relationship with God—through which man reaches ultimate reality and thereby achieves true immortality. Religion is a state of being, not a ritualized performance. The Bible says: "I hate, I despise your feasts" (Amos 5:21). Religion is not ritual, for ritual has more concern for the performance, but true religion gets to the essence of life.

"Even though you offer me your burnt offerings and cereal offerings,
  I will not accept them . . .
But let justice roll down like waters,
  and righteousness like an everflowing stream."

Amos 5:22, 24

True religion is not evidenced by Gothic cathedrals, but it can sometimes be viewed when radical youth shout objections to the existing order. Religion is feeding the poor and clothing the naked. Religion is not moving up the social scale from Pentecostal to Presbyterian, in a single generation; it is the deep force within us that gets the best out of us and makes us reach for the highest life we can attain. Religion is the spontaneous prayer when our children are born, and when our parents die, and when we make another attempt toward love, because hate keeps us out of touch with ultimate reality, which is God.

And true morality is a component of true religion, but is sometimes hard to detect. False concepts of morality have been so ingrained into our thinking that it is hard to tell the genuine from the imitation. Morality is not flag waving, and it is not flag burning. It has nothing to do with playing cards or dancing or smoking cigarettes, for you can be a non-card player, a non-dancer, a non-drinker, and a non-cigarette smoker and still be out of touch with God. But morality has to do with truth, and any compromise with truth becomes immorality!

In his book *My Bondage and My Freedom,* Frederick Douglass, self-liberated from slavery, spoke the truth ten years before emancipation to a hostile world that did not believe him to be a man because he was Black.

At an early age, in good Socratic tradition, Douglass began to question his world. *"Why am I a slave?"* he asked. He had been told that God was good, but now he began to question God and the people who professed to know the thoughts of God. Douglass said:

> I found that there were puzzling exceptions to this theory of slavery on both sides, and in the middle. I knew of blacks who were *not* slaves; I knew of whites who were *not* slaveholders; and I knew of persons who were *nearly* white, who were slaves. *Color,* therefore, was a very unsatisfactory basis for slavery. . . .
>
> It was not *color,* but *crime;* not *God,* but *man;* that afforded the true explanation of the existence of slavery; nor was I long in finding out another important truth, viz: what man can make, man can unmake. The appalling darkness faded away, and I was master of the subject.[1]

This is Douglass's existential self-affirmation of authentic courage to be. Paul Tillich has said:

> The courage to be as oneself is the courage to follow reason and to defy irrational authority. . . . [It] is not a resigned courage to be. It dares not only to face the vicissitudes of fate and the inescapability of death but to affirm itself as transforming reality according to the demands of reason. It is a fighting, daring courage.[2]

And this has been the crux, the fire, the towering mission of the Black church. Through vicissitude after vicissitude, it has been the marching phalanx of our freedom—the torch of our hope and the flame of our liberty.

The foundation of the Black church is laid in the innermost depth of the Black man's anxiety as evidenced by his songs and his progress in his striving to be free. Frederick Douglass says in *My Bondage and My Freedom:*

> "I did not, when a slave, understand the deep meanings of those rude, and apparently incoherent songs. I was myself within the circle, so that I neither saw nor heard as those without might see and hear. They told me a tale which was then altogether beyond my feeble comprehension; they were tones, loud, long and deep, breathing the prayer and complaint of souls boiling over with the bitterest anguish. Every tone was a

[1] Frederick Douglass, *My Bondage and My Freedom* (New York: Dover Publication, Inc., 1969), p. 90.

[2] Paul Tillich, *The Courage to Be* (New Haven: Yale University Press, 1952), p. 116.

testimony against slavery, and a prayer to God for deliverance from chains." [3]

Just as the religion of the Jews was conceived during their enslavement in Egypt and their journey through the wilderness, so the religion of the Blacks in this continent was born in anxiety; they were a nation within a nation, who adapted the feats and exploits of the Jews for their own purposes in their own idiom. They created spirituals such as "Didn't My Lord Deliver Daniel?" and "Swing Low Sweet Chariot," coming to carry me home, not to heaven but to Freedom Land.

Through this kind of seemingly crude religion the community was established through the interdependence of souls related in an invisible, intangible spirit. "Primitive" people were able to reach beyond the obvious, and with strategic use of emotion they became individuals intuitively united, providing strength for the whole. According to Carl Jung it is not the rational, but the extra-rational, that accounts for religion. This force stems from deep within the subconsciousness of all mankind and unites men in their quest for ultimate reality. The songs and progress and faith of our Black ancestors, my brothers and sisters, made us survive; without it we would have died. And this has kept us surviving to this day.

The fundamental art of the Black church is found not only in music, but in poetry, too. Our poems are our prayers, unwritten but "offered from the heart." And our prayers are still to be heard on prayer meeting night in the Black churches of the North and South.

Typical of these is one "taken down" and preserved by James Weldon Johnson.

> O Lord, we come this morning
> Knee-bowed and body-bent
> Before thy throne of grace.
> O Lord—this morning—
> Bow our hearts beneath our knees,
> And our knees in some lonesome valley.
> We come this morning—
> Like empty pitchers to a full fountain,
> With no merits of our own.
> O Lord—open up a window of heaven,

[3] Douglass, *op. cit.,* p. 99.

> And lean out far over the battlements of glory,
> And listen this morning.[4]

And of the Black preacher whom Black-conscious youth of today are apt to scorn, James Weldon Johnson says:

He has been portrayed only as a semi-comic figure. He had, it is true, his comic aspects, but on the whole he was an important figure, and at bottom a vital factor. It was through him that the people of diverse languages and customs who were brought here from diverse parts of Africa and thrown into slavery were given their first sense of unity and solidarity. He was the first shepherd of this bewildered flock. His power for good or ill was very great. It was the old-time preacher who for generations was the mainspring of hope and inspiration for the Negro in America. . . .

They [old-time Negro preachers] were all saturated with the sublime phraseology of the Hebrew prophets and steeped in the idioms of King James English, so when they preached and warmed to their work, they spoke another language, a language far removed from traditional Negro dialect.[5]

And he is still the main hope of the race, for the hope of the race rests with the Black working masses, and the voice of the Black preacher still remains the only real voice that the Black masses will heed with continuing confidence.

The early Black revolutionaries were preachers of the violent variety. Revolts were conceived and executed because their leaders knew that slavery was wrong. Spirituals tell the story:

> Go down, Moses,
> Way down in Egypt land,
> Tell old Pharaoh,
> Let my people go.

> Oh Freedom, oh Freedom;
> Oh Lord, freedom over me,
> And before I'd be a slave,
> I'll be buried in my grave,
> And go home to my God and be free.

The slaves based their right to protest by revolt on scriptural

[4] James Weldon Johnson, *God's Trombones* (New York: The Viking Press, Inc., 1969), p. 13. Copyright 1927 by The Viking Press, Inc., renewed 1955 by Grace Nail Johnson. All rights reserved. Reprinted by permission of The Viking Press, Inc.

[5] James Weldon Johnson, *op. cit.,* pp. 2, 9.

authority. Such a preacher revolutionary was Denmark Vesey, who was fascinated by the eschatological imagery of the Old Testament, Joshua 6:21: "Then they utterly destroyed all in the city, both men and women, young and old, oxen, sheep, and asses, with the edge of the sword." This was his evidence that the Bible advocated revolt.

Nat Turner was a runaway slave who believed that he was divinely destined to lead the slaves in rebellion. The Black Prophet, as he was known to the slaves, heard a voice which told him that the Serpent was loosed, Christ had laid down the yoke, that he, Nat, was to take it up again, and the time was fast approaching when the first should be last and the last should be first.

And Paul Tillich says: "The pole of individualization expresses itself in the religious experience as a personal encounter with God." [6]

It seems obvious that early Black preacher-revolutionaries displayed Paul Tillich's courage of the Reformer. They had a confidence derived from a personal encounter with God—because from no other source could one secure sanction (in the same way that Moses secured sanction) for the purpose.

According to Tillich, the courage of the Reformer is not simply courage to be oneself—or the courage to be as a part. "It transcends and unites both of them. For the courage of confidence is not rooted in confidence about oneself. . . . It is threatened neither by the loss of oneself nor by the loss of one's world." [7]

The authenticity of the Black church cannot be established in a sermon as brief as this. There will still be dissent about its role and relevance, about its illicit preachers, its hypocrites, its outmoded rules, its money raising, its guilt, its sense of segregation that still displeases the Black rejectors. Even in spite of the perennial questions "What is wrong?" and "How much is wrong?" still the church has been and continues to be the most formidable force for freedom the Black man has. And the more we move from the church, the worse off the race will get. The further we move from the Bible, the worse our schools will get. The further we move from Jesus, the worse our children will get.

[6] Tillich, *op. cit.,* p. 160.
[7] *Ibid.,* p. 163.

Perhaps we need a collective self-affirmation to lose our sense of alienation from God and from our brothers. With a true sense of the courage to be in harmony with God and with our brother, alienation can be transformed to art, to music, to poetry and prose, and to constructive action.

To be sure, I know the weakness and inadequacies of the Black church. I know that in these days we often seem to have lost our courage, lost our vision, lost our spirit. But our courage is not lost; perhaps we have not used it as we ought to, but it is not lost. Our vision is not lost. The same God who gave vision to Moses, to Abraham and Isaac and Jacob—and to the great Black Christian leaders of the past—still rules. We need only let God lead us. The great power of the church that kept our families together, and that made our people honest and decent and helpful to each other, is not dead. If we will tarry in prayer, God will give us power from on high. And the Holy Spirit is not dead. He is still with us: and if we will let him come in, the Spirit will help us to overcome all things. Jesus has not forsaken us. Open the door of our lives and let him in!

Perhaps there is one of you with the courage of the pragmatic reformer who will set our church in order, starting with yourself —getting love in your heart, getting prejudice and envy and hate out of your heart, letting the Holy Spirit come into your life, starting with yourself. Perhaps some young Moses, who will lead our people as a servant of God to the Promised Land, is listening today, who will find a way that will ultimately help reunite all mankind.

2
YOUTH—
FROM DROPOUTS
TO DROPINS

The development of our youth is our salvation of the race. We can assess the problems of the future of the race and of the nation on the basis of things that are happening to our young people. The major emphasis of the church must of necessity be pointed toward youth, not only for the preservation of the church as an institution but also for the promulgation of the call of Christ to witness in the nation and around the world. We cannot build the future on the old distorted ideas concerning youth.

Jesus alluded to this when he warned against putting new wine into old wineskins (Luke 5:37-38). We who are older have had our day for the most part. That day has not been very bright. Barriers and problems have plagued our way. The focus, therefore, of the church is also the focus of my work as a Christian minister. I saw, first of all, the needs of youth. These needs were evident when I arrived in New York in 1943 to serve as a supply minister of Rendall Presbyterian Church in Harlem on 136th St. near Lenox Ave. The late Jesse Jai McNeil speaks of this concern that I had:

The preacher-prophet's concern with the moral and spiritual problems of organized human life reaches back to the settling of the Israelite clans in the hill country of Canaan and their eventual coalescence with the Amorites who inhabited the walled cities in the lowlands of this new land into which the Israelites had come. The Israelite clans came out of the desert conditioned by and committed to a kinship or brother-justice. The circumstances of nomadic life had taught them the necessity of holding a given territory or district as a common possession, of moving about together in search of food or for purposes of defense, and of sharing the fortune or misfortune of the clan as a common lot.[1]

This was the starting point of my ministry in New York when I was only twenty-one years of age. I majored in the concerns of the youth.

There were no organized programs in Harlem dealing with problems of juvenile delinquency over and beyond what was done by the YMCA, YWCA, and some small-scale efforts by churches, boys' clubs, and similar organizations. Something more had to be done to bring to the folks of the total community the need for developing their youth mentally, physically, and spiritually. I therefore began to work with small groups, organizing baseball, softball, and basketball teams. I also converted a large dance hall, then known as the Golden Gate, into a youth center in the middle of Harlem. The auditorium was used for a vast basketball court. Sometimes as many as three hundred people at a time engaged in recreational activities in this transformed dance hall.

I saw many things happen in Harlem. I saw a gang war and I saw the results of gang war—slain boys. I saw the beginning of the dope traffic which has become a problem throughout America. This happened before we recognized that of all of our young people, particularly those living in the poverty sections, were subject to all kinds of illicit and criminal activities.

I also could see, particularly in the Black community, that there was lacking a unified, cohesive home experience. Often there was no father at home at all. The mother had to work

[1] Jesse Jai McNeil, *The Preacher-Prophet in Mass Society* (Grand Rapids: Wm. B. Eerdmans Publishing Co., 1961), p. 67.

in order to keep the family together. The children therefore were left to roam the streets to take care of themselves. We called them "key" children because they carried their house keys hanging from their necks. These children were susceptible to all the main problems of that concentrated community. Mary Ellen Goodman alludes to this kind of situation.

> Charles "runs wild" on a street dense with children, most of them Negroes.
> "There's nowhere else for him to play," his mother tells us, "but he sure hears all kinds of things and gets awful beat up by the big boys. He's got scars all over him. Just last week a Brown boy about seven hit him in the head with a brick. We had to get it sewed up, it was so bad. . . ." [2]

I began to form block organizations in Harlem under the name of "coordinated councils of juvenile aid." This effort developed into a network of precincts organized against juvenile delinquency. While I was working with the police and with these community groups, we developed what we called, even then, a model of self-determination in community problems.

When I left New York and went to New Jersey to become pastor of the First Baptist Church of South Orange, of course, I began to serve a small church in a much smaller community. I left New York because my wife felt that the big cities were doing more harm than good and that they were losing contact with God. I also needed to have my feet on the ground to get a direction for the rest of my life.

Almost as soon as I arrived in South Orange, I began again to work with the young people. I helped in the development of athletic competitions, educational programs, and other activities. As I continued to experiment with meeting the needs of youth in the church, I realized that the church could not be a one-day affair, the prayer meeting or Sunday school session alone; it had to offer a day-by-day program which would really supplement the public schools.

[2] Mary Ellen Goodman, *Race Awareness in Young Children* (New York: Collier Books, 1964), p. 152.

Youth is really a critical period of life. The lives of youth cannot be reached just by talking. Something had to be done in South Orange to gear them into some form of participatory activity which they could enjoy, one in which they could see the relationship between God's goodness and what they were doing.

After five years in South Orange I was ready to demonstrate what I believed God had prepared me to do.

I responded to the call of the Zion Baptist Church in Philadelphia, the oldest Black Baptist church in the north section of Philadelphia. This church had a reputation for vital and enlightened progressive membership. Here I would be able to move forward and test my hopes and my plans in a pragmatic way.

When I arrived in Philadelphia, I found that although no more than 25 percent of the population was Black, the greatest number of those accused of juvenile delinquency were in the Black community. Before the Second World War parents had exerted closer control over their young people. However, now there was a large influx of migrants into Philadelphia, as into New York and Newark and the other large metropolitan areas, due to increasing defense jobs and other employment opportunities. As I visited homes where the man was off to war or to work and the mother was away at work or someplace else, I could see the development on a broad scale of the kind of thing I had seen in Harlem where the child was out on the street by himself with the key around his neck. There he was making his own way with no guiding hand to direct him or to lead him and no voice to inspire him: he was helpless. Every child needs a home! There were no friends in the neighborhood who would help. In the smaller communities "back home" when the father and mother were away, there would be several in the neighborhood who knew the child well enough to exert some influence in his life. But in the big city, with the new influx of people who did not know each other, moving from house to house in the same neighborhood, there was usually not even one neighbor who knew the child well enough to exert much influence in that child's life.

Children began to run wild, not only in the so-called poor neighborhoods but in the so-called better neighborhoods, too. In striving for better homes or a better way of life, the mothers and fathers found it necessary to hold not one but two jobs, thus leaving the child in a nice house with soft rugs and plush furniture, yet unattended, unguided. There was no voice that could serve to give the love and direction necessary to develop a child so he or she could relate in a positive way to his or her everyday experiences. The child left idle after school often got into trouble, not because he was a natural-born trouble-maker but simply because children gathering on street corners can easily become involved in things that will create problems. They are wide open to anything that might come along to fill their emptiness. In order that the child may feel a part of his group and be able to attain a respected position of recognition, he needs love, security, recognition, and achievement. Yet these are missing ingredients in many young lives—especially in the lives of "key" children!

Seeing that the Black community had this problem (although I found it in the White community as well), I made it my principal focus. I concluded that I must gear my ministry to help young people find themselves and, in doing so, to find their God. I believe that in finding God even a child could find himself.

Therefore I began with the same old pattern that I had used from the very beginning in my ministry. Having been an athlete, I began organizing athletic teams. Having been interested in dramatics, I began organizing dramatic groups. I also began to organize literary groups and many other kinds of active youth groups.

In the area where my church then stood I sought to widen my ministry beyond that of the church building. I helped in the development of adult youth councils to fight the causes of juvenile delinquency in our city. Out of this activity grew the Philadelphia Citizens' Committee on Juvenile Delinquency. We organized scores of Black organizations in the early fifties in Philadelphia. This effort was used by many other cities as a pattern for the organization of citizen participation in programs to fight the causes of delinquency among juveniles.

While working with young people in this context, I saw the necessity for job opportunities for youth because over and over again I heard them talk about discrimination. I saw young people finish college who could not get a simple clerk's job in a small business or in a public industry. I met young men with brilliant minds who could not go far simply because they were Black, although they received all kinds of excuses from personnel offices as to why they were kept from job opportunities.

It was then that I personally began to communicate with presidents and to check with boards of businesses and corporations in Philadelphia asking them to have their personnel departments just interview several of the Blacks. I hoped and believed that this effort would open some good jobs to these deserving young people, but I received few responses. I wrote the mayor of the city and the governor of the state; I talked with members of the commission on human relations, but always I received only a courtesy reply or a "Well, we are doing the best we can; we will try harder," or "Nothing can be done about the situation now," or "You can't push too hard; it takes time to open these doors."

Well, I have read the Bible where Jesus said: "All things are possible to him who believes" (Mark 9:23). Another time he said, "Ask, and it will be given you; seek, and you will find; knock, and it will be opened to you" (Matthew 7:7). So I decided that it was time to test the Bible and to test God in this crucial problem that affected Black children in Philadelphia in particular and in America in general. I would not depend on the mayor, the governor, or even the president of the United States to solve the problem of job opportunities for Blacks. Here in Philadelphia we would demonstrate what the church of God could do itself, utilizing its own strength, its own power, its children of God, through the utilization of simple purchasing power. We would withhold our patronage from those firms that would not employ our people.

I had learned that the profit margin of many industries was so narrow that the removal of a block of patronage by a sizable number of a city's population would be sufficient to run even the best of the companies into bankruptcy. It was not my desire to run companies into bankruptcy, because I wanted to see the continuation of free enterprise. I have nothing against free enterprise. I believe that free enterprise is the best way to economic prosperity that I know of in the world today. It is the best of economic systems for economic prosperity and economic opportunity. The problem is that the free enterprise system as we knew it was free enterprise for the White people and not for the Black people. Democracy is the greatest system of government in the world. The only problem with democracy in America is that it does not work for Black people. If we could get democracy to work for all people, regardless of color, democracy would unquestionably be the greatest political and governmental experiment ever witnessed in the history of mankind. There would be no need for concern about communism, because historical and dialectical materialism cannot hold a light to a democratic system that is real and true and fulfills the full meaning of democracy. The basic purpose of our selective patronage was to aid Afro boys and girls in the community. This move was the first step of the ladder of advancement.

This effort was necessary in those days for developing self-dignity and self-ability. Later America would learn that color must not be a requisite for the employment of a boy or girl, a man or woman. We still have a long, long way to go, but at least a breach has now been made, and the first step has been reached in the quest of economic emancipation of Black people.

I had also become aware that many Blacks were dropping out of society. Dope, crime, gang wars, and many so-called antisocial acts were manifestations of this plague of the Black community. Many were willing to write about the problems in the Black community. Andrew Billingsley stated:

> But both formally and informally, the wider society—that is to say, the white society—has held the keys to the survival and prosperity of Negro families and the achievement of family members. Families cannot meet their responsibilities unless the necessary resources and supports are provided by that society, including particularly the economic, health, educational, political, and other subsystems of the society.[3]

E. Franklin Frazier wrote about the situation in Chicago, which was not greatly different from what I saw in Philadelphia:

> The Negro, like other groups marked off from the general population because of color and low economic and cultural status, has found a dwelling-place in the deteriorated area just outside the Loop. In the zone nearest the center of the city, the juvenile delinquency rate, based upon arrests, was over 40 percent. From a physical standpoint this area showed extreme deterioration and gave evidence of the expansion of the central business district. On the one hand, there were dilapidated houses carrying signs of rooms for rent at fifteen and twenty cents a bed, junk shops, markets with stale meat, and crowded Negro quarters with filthy bedding half-visible through sooty and broken window panes. On the other hand, new motorcar salesrooms furnished signs of the future role which the regenerated area would play in the organization of the city. In keeping with the general character of the area, all organized community life had disappeared, and the inhabitants were, on the whole, remnants of broken families and foot-loose men and women.[4]

Claude Brown has characterized the utter hopelessness of the situation, since the manchild was already in the promised land.[5] We Blacks could understand the meaning of dropout.

I decided that something must be done. I wanted a program that would provide for the youth to drop in. In 1953

[3] Andrew Billingsley, *Black Families in White America* (Englewood Cliffs, N.J.: Prentice-Hall, Inc., 1968), p. 99.

[4] E. Franklin Frazier, *The Negro Family in the United States* (Chicago: The University of Chicago Press, 1966), pp. 278-279.

[5] See Claude Brown, *Manchild in the Promised Land* (New York: The Macmillan Company, 1966).

I had been involved in the organization of the North Philadelphia Youth, Community and Employment Services (NPYCES) which was formed to cope with increasing delinquency and juvenile crime in our predominantly Black community of a city consisting at that time of 2,000,000 persons.

The NPYCES attacked the cause-and-effect relationship between delinquency and juvenile crime on the one hand, and between unemployment and unemployability on the other by trying to find jobs for Negro youths. Impetus to the NPYCES was provided by a subsequently organized Selective Patronage Campaign designed to force Philadelphia industrial and business enterprises to open their employment doors to Afro-Americans.

During the first five years of NPYCES' operation, only 5,000 of the 35,000 youths interviewed were placed in jobs; the other 30,000 lacked basic skills, had adverse personal qualities, and/or did not have enough education to obtain work. The failure to place these youths, most of whom existed in abject poverty, pointed up the need for a training facility which would cost trainees little or nothing and would ignore academic entrance requirements.

Philadelphia is a booming, prosperous community: Overall, corporate income and capital expenditures are at record highs; wages and salaries are good; construction of all kinds continues to increase; basic private demand, as evidenced by retail sales and installment buying, is strong. But Philadelphia, despite favorable economic indicators, is a depressed area for at least 450,000 citizens, 390,000 of them Negroes. In sharp contrast to the broader community's prosperity, this sector of the city is plagued with chronic unemployment, underemployment, poverty, and related problems.

The city, according to 1960 census data, housed 46% of the metropolitan area population, which included most of the area's semiskilled and unskilled workers. About 27% of Philadelphia's half-million families had annual incomes of less than $4,000. This meant that one out of every two nonwhite families, as compared to one out of every five White families, was poor. Nonwhites, mainly Negroes, constituted about 25% of the city's male labor force of 532,000; yet they accounted for about 41% of the unemployed. About 33% of the 133,000 nonwhite males in the labor force were classified in the service or laboring groups. Only 12% of the White males were similarly classified.

The disparity between prosperous Philadelphia and depressed Philadelphia is also reflected in the low educational level of the poor. In 1960 over 40,000 Philadelphians twenty-five years of age and older had never been to school. An additional 511,000 had less than an eighth-grade education. And one out of every two nonwhite adults had never reached high school. A study of 3,000 current Philadelphia high school graduates showed that only 14% of Negro graduates (men and women) were enrolled in college. In contrast, 55% of White graduates (men and women) were enrolled in college.

Faced with these conditions, Black leadership in Philadelphia's civil rights movement—still strongly influenced by Black ministers and their congregations—realized that the ending of discriminatory hiring practices would still leave thousands of unemployed with such barriers to employment as the following:

- Lack of skill training
- Inadequate basic education
- Inadequate personal and social skills
- Lack of motivation and self-interest

It was apparent that no existing institution in Philadelphia, public or private, was equipped to help this target population to overcome these barriers; therefore, no amount of protest against the "power structure" would produce any immediate results.

Faced with these conditions, we organized the Opportunities Industrialization Center (OIC) more as an extension of the civil rights movement than as a school—and based more on faith and inspiration than on theory.

There persists the belief among the OIC leadership that no amount of money poured into a community can help beyond a certain level unless the people who live there are inspired and motivated first to help themselves. In order to implement the concept of self-help, the operating program of OIC developed unique techniques in recruitment, intake, and orientation; it created the Feeder Program, vocational occupational skills training, Adult Armchair Education, placement, evaluation, and follow-up. Let us examine the various parts of the program.

From the beginning, the OIC recruitment policy has sought to bring the poorly equipped residents of the poverty areas into the program. However, in lieu of a large recruitment staff, OIC has established close relationships with churches, public health centers, social worker groups, labor unions, Neighborhood Youth Corps, the City Civil Service Commission, community action councils, and the State Department of Public Assistance in order to reach those in need. The local employment service office has also been utilized. OIC recruitment is a strenuous effort to develop face-to-face contacts in such centers as barber shops, bars, beauty parlors, and poolrooms, and also on the street.

Under a recently revised recruitment structure, the OIC has also developed a recruiting program through companies themselves. The companies are asked to refer to OIC those individuals with marginal skills whom the personnel officers in the companies have rejected for employment. This has become an increasingly important source for recruiting. Typically, the OIC people were quick to recognize that by establishing this relationship they could also reap the advantage of establishing a closer relationship with a particular firm with a view to placement at a later date.

In the early phase, April through June, 1965, over 26 percent of the enrollees were under twenty-one years of age. In December, 1966, the proportion was 27.3 percent. During the period of April through June, 1965, approximately 16 percent of the enrollees had eight years or less of educational background; by December, 1966, this proportion had shrunk to approximately 9 percent. OIC has been singularly successful in attracting Negro males into the program. Early in the OIC operation, during the period April through June, 1965, only 41 percent of the enrollees were males, but this figure grew to 62.7 percent by May, 1972.

After an intake procedure, which includes the intake interview and the referral, the individual is moved into the Feeder Program with a minimum of delay. The idea has been to move the recruit as quickly as possible into a situation which he sees as getting him underway in the development of a new career. Prior to the Feeder Program itself, there is an orientation process involving four sessions that last from one to three hours, consisting essentially of an attempt to provide the motivational reinforcement of OIC. These sessions are scheduled each month with both day and evening hours. This motivational emphasis is followed by discussions about the various skill-training areas by the appropriate instructors. A description and explanation of the OIC rules, regulations, and general behavioral requirements, as well as an outline of what will be taking place in the Feeder Program itself, is made quite clear during the orientation program. Motivation for self-improvement is the most important key to the success of the Feeder Program and to the real success of OIC.

The basic philosophy of the skill training program at OIC has been to design programs with specific employers in mind. In addition, employer involvement has been sought and obtained in the form of equipment donation and representation on the technical-advisory committees.

From the outset there has been a strong emphasis on curriculum development performed in concert with the actual employers themselves. For example, in the teletype class, the machines on which the trainees learn are the specialized equipment used by Western Union. In addition, the course has been designed by Western Union staff people. This degree of specificity varies between the various skill-training programs.

In the early stages of OIC development, some of the equipment contributed by various business firms was obsolescent or second-rate in various ways. However, on the basis of successful training programs and an impressive overall OIC program, the business community commitment has responded with more meaningful contributions.

Starting with ten courses in Philadelphia in 1964, OICs across America now provide over 225 classes of training for more than forty occupations.

OIC's successful job placement is due to its initial approach to the business and industrial community for technical and financial help in the formative stage of the program. Sold on the concept of self-help and the opportunity to become involved in structuring courses to the particular labor needs of various corporations, industry contributed $200,000 worth of equipment, furniture, teaching aids, and other materials necessary to establish the program.

Financial support was immediate from unions, fraternal groups, civic and church groups, and individuals. This strong support has continued. For example, when OIC began, its first large support outside of the churches came from the Philadelphia-based Haas Community Fund, and when OIC's request for funds for a Spanish-speaking Developmental Center was turned down by OEO, the money was supplied by Smith Kline and French. Ninety-eight percent of the equipment used has been donated by industry, and requests for OIC trainees continue to come from industries closely involved. Some classes are closed out and the trainees are placed on jobs before the course is completed. This is done at the specific request of employers.

Initial contacts, however, have been supplemented by job promotional efforts now concentrated in the communities surrounding the centers. These complement the work of the Job Development Specialists on each staff. Community residents and business leaders have been invited to serve on OIC boards.

As the fame of the Philadelphia OIC spread, individuals and groups from all over the nation wanted to come and see. Almost always after the visit, the next question was: how can our community do likewise? Rev. Gus Roman, who worked with the Extension Services, traveled all across America talking about OIC as a new kind of program of hope and faith.

Letters, telephone calls, and visitors poured into Philadelphia. To take care of this public interest, the OIC Institute was established. It:

- Answers letters of inquiry
- Schedules tours of the Philadelphia operations for visiting delegations
- Provides advice for communities that are exploring the possibilities of setting up OIC locals
- Renders technical assistance to communities that have organized themselves for locally funded OICs
- Assists community financed OICs in exploring possibilities of federal and/or philanthropic assistance
- Helps potential and operational OIC locals in the selection and orientation of staff and board of directors

The Institute seeks to serve as a channel of information and suggestion between OIC operatives and the interested public. It is set up to provide local centers with good technical assistance on a continuing basis. The technical capability of the Institute has been enhanced by the rigid selection of staff to administer the work program. The concept of regionalization is not new to the Institute. For each region a *team* is responsible for making available the required technical assistance. The team is able to service all of the crucial technical needs of a local OIC, such as outreach, instruction, program development, counseling, testing, placement, board-staff relations, and general and fiscal management. The team serves as a technical assistance bank that might be drawn upon whenever needed. The team has a regional director, who has knowledge of the types of problems that an OIC executive director deals with daily and can direct the team as a comprehensive resource for problem solution. He must explain federal positions, regulations, and directives, and the need for compliance with them. He is responsible for assuring action on technical assistance plans and for advising on changes. Also there are field specialists on the team, each offering expertise in one of or a combination of the following clusters of specialties:

- Counseling, testing, and recruitment
- Vocational education
- Adult basic education
- Job development and follow-up
- Fiscal management and administration

The team is responsible for technical assistance, the utilization of consultants, mobilization of local technical assistance resources, reporting to federal agencies, and the implementation of a staff-training program.

The OIC National Institute was founded out of a dramatic demand created by public interest. It is the birthplace of new OIC expansion, the delivery room for new self-help programs throughout the country.

Long before the National Institute goes to work providing technical guidance for the establishment of an OIC facility, the Extension Services personnel have already done considerable pioneering work. This is an organization that goes into various urban and rural areas throughout the country and determines whether the climate is right for the establishment of an OIC organization.

Through continued assistance and consultation, the OIC extension staff develops, in local communities, the capability for interested groups to organize and successfully operate an OIC job-training center. Upon reaching a reasonable level of maturity, the local OIC is recommended to the OIC "Allocation and Review Committee," for support through a unique bulk-funding arrangement with federal manpower and poverty programs. This Allocation and Review Committee is composed of a rotating group of OIC board chairmen and executive directors. This plan represents "revenue sharing" at its best.

The Extension Services check community interests. They look at the community's need for skills. They inventory local leadership. In general, they accumulate a great deal of information which helps them in making recommendations as to whether an OIC could best fit the needs of a particular community.

In addition, OIC can be an important vehicle for generating voluntary self-help efforts for community improvement. Because it is the only national manpower program developed by indigenous community leaders, OIC has had, and will undoubtedly continue to have, great appeal to those seeking an outlet for self-help efforts. Each OIC board of directors represents a cross section of the local community and offers a high degree of community participation in program planning and control. The normal practice of adding former trainees to local boards on a rotating basis insures full participation by those most affected by the operation of OIC.

The Extension Services arm has proved to be a valuable forerunner in the establishment of OIC installations. It is an essential step in the total OIC approach.

The experience gained in helping local communities organize job-training centers gives the OIC extension staff a valuable resource for fulfilling the potential for OIC expansion. With only a modest expansion of staff resources, the OIC Extension Department could double the number of existing OIC centers in any given year.

In an attempt to meet the need for leadership, a management training program was established in the OIC Institute. This program was designed to provide administrative training for persons destined to become leaders in the local OIC programs. They were to become acquainted with the OIC history and philosophy, manpower and good general management practices. The Management Training School was established because of the obvious need for more highly trained executive directors, deputies, chiefs of training in feeder and skills counseling and job and program developing throughout the OIC world.

The OIC Management Training School carries out a vigorous program to train executive directors and then deputies, as well as other key staff people. Management training also can provide basic training for members of boards of directors.

Generally speaking, persons attending the Management Training School are selected on the basis of sincerity, training, intelligence, and capacity to learn. Equally important is the individual's manifested sense of confidence in and his commitment to the OIC philosophy and objectives—that self-help is of primary importance in resolving the needs of the economically disadvantaged.

Persons have come to the Management Training School from all over the country in order to participate in the three-month course. The course includes principles of management, fiscal management, basic contracts, labor relations, basic principles of civil law, and basic business practices. In addition, the philosophy of OIC is taught and demonstrated. The participants are also trained in all phases of OIC operations and spend some time in the prototype (Philadelphia OIC).

The staff which carries out the program includes, in addition to the Management Training School staff, members of the staff of the OIC National Institute, the Philadelphia OIC, Wharton School of Finance, Temple University, and leading industries. Persons completing the program insure OIC of an adequate number of trained and talented people well qualified to manage the variety of tasks required by the uniqueness of OIC.

OIC's potential for rational and orderly expansion has been greatly strengthened by the organization of the National OIC Industrial Advisory Council, composed of top executives from thirty of the major business corporations in the nation, led by George Champion, of the Chase Manhattan Bank. By providing continuous consultation, the Council offers a vital link to the industrial community that will insure a high standard of performance by OIC, especially in keeping the job training relevant to projected manpower needs. The solid support of the top business firms in the nation, unparalleled in any other manpower program, offers clear testimony to the faith in OIC's potential for the future.

Financial and management services provided on the national level include:

- A professional auditing function for the entire network
- A systems and measurement approach to managing the network of OICs
- Liaison with the federal government
- Liaison with the Industrial Advisory Council
- A clearing house for OIC personnel
- Public information

Through continued staff training and managerial development, OIC has built a cadre of talented executives whose knowledge and experience greatly reduce waste in the expenditure of government and private funds, which often stems more from the lack of experience than from any other elements. The present Executive Director of the OIC Institute, Frederick Miller, is a master at OIC organizational techniques and he is assisted by Elton Jolly, also a man of fine abilities.

Throughout its existence OIC has attracted high-caliber administrators with deep motivation and dedication to the OIC philosophy. The focus of all management efforts, including the planning, organization, and operation of OIC centers, is the trainee. Interpersonal differences and administrative conflicts tend to decline when an organization staff perceives a singular purpose and develops the determination to provide service to those for whom OIC was established.

The potential of OIC, as with any other growing organization, can be seriously impaired if there is no mechanism for continuing follow-up and evaluation of program performance. Post-placement follow-up serves two purposes. It is the means by which the OIC staff learns how employees evaluate the effectiveness of trainees. It is also the means by which contact with former trainees is continued. Meaningful feedback from a follow-up system provides a vital source of information for shaping future curricula offerings and for selecting trainees for job placement.

OIC has been tried successfully—experimented with and demonstrated with—since 1964 in all types of urban situations, metropolitan, medium-sized, and where a small town may be the capital of surrounding counties, and in all parts of the country from Boston to Jacksonville to Dallas to Seattle.

Certain distinctive characteristics of it have been individual self-help, neighborhood leadership, total community support, "hard sell" recruiting, psychological reconditioning, identification of instructor with trainee, maximum feasible participation in vocational choice, organizational decision making, and community support.

Dr. Maurice Dawkins, valued Executive Vice-Chairman of the OIC National work, interprets OIC goals to government, congressional representatives, and to the American community at large, including church groups. The participation of churches and ministers is, and must remain, an integral part of the OIC movement. Without that participation OIC would become just another bureaucracy, or community organization, and would lose its purpose and spirit. OIC was born in the church, and that support is essential to its survival and effectiveness.

OIC has led to a cooperative effort among a wide variety of agencies and individuals in public and private sectors.

In a telegram to me, President Richard M. Nixon made the following statement:

Last September [1968], at the impressive new Progress Plaza Shopping Center in Philadelphia, I had the opportunity to tell you of my great commitment to the self-help goals of OIC. If you recall, we shook hands on this commitment. It was a firm handshake. This week, at my request,

you had luncheon with my assistant for urban affairs, Daniel Patrick
Moynihan, and he renewed the pledge of my administration to cooperate
fully in the aims and aspirations of OIC.

I salute the work your organizations have done in the past and look
forward to working closely with you in the years ahead.

The New Morality
and the Church
A SERMON

"You will know the truth and the truth will make you free."—*John 32:8*

Today an awesome spirit of terrifying proportions is sweeping across America and the Western world. It is the spirit of moral decay and moral degeneracy. It is a spirit that has gotten deep into the fiber of the home, deep into the fiber of the community, deep into the fiber even of the church, and it affects both the young and the old. It is a spirit that has been seen before in the history of other civilizations, other nations, and other cultures. It is the spirit of human degeneracy that has destroyed every great civilization, prior to our own, that did not resist it.

It was this spirit of moral decay and degeneracy that destroyed the Roman Empire. Rome was not destroyed by the Huns, or by the Goths, the Franks, or the Gauls. These barbarians, as they were called, were merely the catalysts for what happened. Long before the barbarians swept down from the North upon the gates of Rome, Rome was already dying from degeneracy and immorality. Likewise did the great civilizations of Persia fall, and those of Egypt, and the great early cultures of the Orient and Northern Africa. All fell because they died first from within. They died from diseases of the mind, diseases of the spirit, and diseases of the flesh.

Unless something is done to stop it soon, that same moral decay, that same moral degeneracy, that same spiritual cancer that destroyed Rome and Persia and Egypt, and other great cultures that once thrived in the world, will destroy America. Moral decay in America is seeping deeper and deeper into all parts of our national culture and our national institutions, deeper and deeper into our homes, our schools, our government, and even our churches.

If we do not halt it within this very century, the great population centers of America like New York City, Chicago, Los Angeles, and Philadelphia will become modern Sodoms and Gomorrahs. Lawlessness, crime, and degeneracy will prevail from the high to the low, from the Black to the White, from the young to the old. A spirit of vast corruption will take over our cities. And God will permit this nation to be destroyed.

To a large measure the problem before us is tied up with the so-called new morality. The church does have a position to take in this matter. If the church did not have a position, it ought to have one, for God is still depending upon his church and upon his preacher and upon his people to save the nation and to redeem the soul of a decaying and dying generation.

The church must concentrate its effort toward pulling together the family and developing the home. All sane sociological analysis recognizes the family as the basic unit of society. All of the institutions we know had their beginnings in the home, from the day that the home was a cave or a shelter in a tree. The home has been the genesis of all our social institutions. The first school was the home. The first teacher was the mother in the home. The first church was the home. The Bible teaches us that religion must be centered first in the home. The home is the main cornerstone for the teaching of spiritual truths and moral values. What happens in the states depends on what happens in the home; what happens in the government depends on what happens in the home. As goes the home, so goes the nation—and so goes the world.

But today we are witnessing the steady erosion of the home life of America among both Black and White. The reason for this breakdown is clear. The mothers and fathers of America have lost the religious perspectives of their elders and have turned away from God. We have turned away from the reading of the Bible. We have turned away from family prayers. We have turned away from a faith to believe in. We have turned away from religion. We no longer believe that we have a need for God, and so we have stopped reading the Bible and praying in our schools, and we have stopped praying in our organizations, and we have stopped praying in our homes with our families, and we have stopped giving honor in our minds to God.

We have become great and prosperous and mighty as a nation. But we have begun to believe that "we did it all by ourselves," forgetting that all we have as a nation has come from God *who lifted us, who blessed us* and *exalted us,* and who made the nation mighty. God has done all this in spite of the hate and the discrimination and the evils we have practiced one against the other. In spite of ourselves, God has made our nation great. But let us not forget that what God has built, God can tear down. For God has told us what to expect whenever we try to build without him. He told us, "Except the Lord build the House they labor in vain that build it."

What we seem to forget is that our God is a God of judgment, as well as a God of love. He can build, but he can also destroy!

It has been in the breakdown of the home that we can see the evidences of the breakdown of the nation. Let us look at some of the startling figures that tell us what is happening in the home life of America.

First, let us look at the divorce statistics. At the end of the Second World War the rate was one divorce to every six marriages in the country. That figure was high enough, but today the record is much worse. Of every three marriages, one of them will end in divorce. Five hundred thousand divorces were granted in the United States last year alone. Today, ten million children are living in homes without a father. Five hundred thousand babies were born to teenage mothers last year, out of wedlock. In Washington, D.C., last year, the increase of babies born to mothers out of wedlock was 1000 percent since 1960. And more disturbing to us is the fact that, though the Afro comprise one-tenth of the American population, still one-third of all the babies born out of wedlock last year were Black. Nine out of ten of all the girls that drop out of school do so because of pregnancy, and many of them cannot tell for sure who the real father is. In Philadelphia most of these girls are Black.

Almost invariably teenage marriages, when they do occur, end up in divorce courts within a year or two after the marriage takes place. Our boys and girls date at ten, go steady at thirteen, get married at seventeen (if they get married), and divorce before they are old enough to vote. In the face of the rising divorce rate and the increasing sexual promiscuity, a marriage that lasts is becoming as obsolete as a Model T Ford. The idea of one man for one woman, *for life,* is becoming a notion of the past.

Undergirding all of this is the new sexual revolution that is the most disturbing and devastating development of all. In the past ten years the Western world, primarily the White man, seems to have discovered sex. Today, we read sex, hear sex, talk sex, and see sex everywhere we go. Of the top twenty songs on the Hit Parade, eighteen of them have sexy titles or sexy lyrics. Of the best selling books in America today, nearly all of them in some form or another deal with sex as the central theme. As a matter of fact, most publishers will not print a decent novel today. Authors know that to get a book published, it must have sex appeal, because they know that the public is buying sex.

The ladies' clothing industry is geared to sex. The designers cut the dresses either to show all that they can at the bottom or to show all that they can at the top.

It is almost impossible for parents to go to a movie today where they can take their children, without being embarrassed by the most vividly erotic and passionate scenes. Television is full of sex, from the morning soap operas to the late-late show. And of the leading commercials, most of them use sex to sell their products: from toilet water to shaving cream. And the situation is getting worse. The prospect is that it will be getting *much* worse. Advertisers have found that sex sells, and they are going to show it as long as it makes money.

With the recent findings of the Commission on Pornography we shall see more exploitation of sex. To be sure there has always been some pornography floating about. When I was a little boy in elementary school in West Virginia, little "dirty paper books" were secretly floating about the school with pictures of nude individuals and couples in compromising positions.

Nudity isn't new. Some of the greatest art in the great museums of the world are nudes, and there is nothing wrong with it as art, for the body is God's greatest work of art. Nothing is more beautiful than a human body artfully portrayed in oils or in stone! But pornography isn't art. Pornography is designed to be filth; it is made to be sold by appealing to the baser senses of the individual. And to say that hard-core pornography does not affect thinking and behavior of young people is an illusion and a lie. It does affect a young person, just as it affects an old person.

The three big factors in a rape are often wine and filthy literature and a demented mind. A young boy gets full of wine, looks at and reads pornography trash, gets a fever in his mind, and

70

goes out and grabs someone to ease his passions. And the one he grabs could be your neighbor, your sister, or your daughter.

Unless something is done to check the flow of filth into our homes, into our schools, and into our communities, the condition will become worse and worse. Something will have to be done to deal with the situation in the nation. It will not be done by the government, nor by Congress, nor by organizations, nor by do-good groups; but in order to do something truly significant about the situation, the church must take the lead. Perhaps it might be necessary for another kind of massive church-wide effort involving ministers and churches of all faiths to concentrate on bringing decency into our communities and getting rid of the piles and piles of smut that are defacing the spirit and the souls of our young people—particularly our Black young people. In our big cities most of the junk written by Whites, printed by Whites, making money for Whites is being poured into our Black communities. We pay for the dirty show and the White man makes the dough!

Through wine, drugs, and filth, the minds of our Black youth are being corrupted more and more every day. No one is going to solve this problem but we ourselves. No one else is going to do it for us. Really, no one else cares that much. For if anything is to be done to deal effectively with these problems, it will have to come from our own people.

The church must therefore establish our directions and decide what the nature of our response will be. First, the church must help to establish a family anchor in an insecure world. The world needs the united home—and the Afro needs the united home more than any other group I know. This is where religion comes in, because only religion can unify the home. There is no other institution in the world that is equal to the occasion. The church is one place where the young and old can join together, around one common cause. The church is the only force which can help solve the prevailing moral and intellectual and spiritual problems of parents and children and society at large.

In a world of change and rebellion, God is the only fixed point that all of us can go to. He is the only one that we can all rally around. Therefore, the church in the future must strive to strengthen and to unify the home, as a main priority.

Second, the church has to consider the whole family in the execution of its program and its work. We must openly challenge the "ways of the world" for the minds and souls of men. The devil is winning out against the church every day, because the church lets him put his program over seven days a week, while we put on our program one day a week, and only for a couple of hours. We have not given the devil much competition. It is no wonder that he seems to be ahead. We cannot beat back the power of Satan by just preaching and shouting on Sundays. Preaching and shouting are all right, but we need to be doing the work of God seven days a week. This is a competitive world, and the church must compete for the lives and souls of men. The devil puts on his light in the bars and cabarets; it is time for the church to put on its light not just outside the buildings, but more so in the hearts and lives of the men and women who *profess* to be Christians—but who fill the bars and cabarets and keep the devil in business.

I am convinced that many of our young people do what they do because they have no substitute for sin. Why do people go to bars? Not just to drink, but also because often they are lonely. They have no one to talk to. Often the only person who will listen to them is the bartender. Many of us Christians don't have time to listen. Successful bartenders know they have to be expert listeners, as well as expert mixers. So people come to talk and to drink and they get drunk. It is not enough for the church to criticize the bars; it must get busy putting something constructive and positive in their place. We will never beat back the devil by talking, because the more we talk about what he does, the more he is going to do. As a matter of fact, we advertise what he does by talking about it so much.

But God's way will win to the extent that we so-called Christian people work in a positive way to provide wholesome weekday social and recreational activities for the youth and the adults of the community, and to the extent that we Christians will get off our high horses and will talk to people who may not have the education that we may have, or live in the big houses some of us may live in. As Christians we must help those who need only some encouragement and a helping hand to stand upon their feet.

We must also get out of our old-fashioned ways and provide social and recreational activities for our young people that will engage their interest and meet their youthful desires.

For example, for years the church has fought against dancing. We have said it was a sin to dance. Now the truth is that most of us danced while we grew up. But now, for our children we say it is a sin to dance. Well—our children are going to dance, whether we like it or not. And I say it is better to let them dance where we can see what they do than to have them hide away in some hole with no light on, to do anything they are big enough to do. We have to become more realistic about the church and the church work and realize that a person can make a sin out of anything; it depends upon how he does it. *Some of us even make a sin out of coming to church,* because we act like the devil when we get here. I don't mind if the children of Zion dance in the church annex across the street, as long as the lights are on and there are chaperons seeing what is going on. As a matter of fact, I would be a chaperon myself if necessary. I would even advocate dancing in the annex as part of a wholesome activity program to engage the interest of our boys and girls.

The church must become a center of activities for adults as well as for the children. We must promote family night and family activities and have more family participation. We must call the whole family to worship now and then, establish family days, and revive the old family-pew worship once in a while, where the whole family can worship together. The whole family should be together in God's house at least sometimes.

The church must strengthen the role of the man in the home. Our homes, particularly our Afro homes, need men. We need men who will gird themselves like men and be strong. We must strengthen the role and the place of the man in the home and in the race. *We must build the male ego!* Maybe our men will stay home more and not find it necessary to run around so much when their role is upgraded in the home to what it ought to be. Building the male ego in our homes will cause our boys growing up to want to be like men, instead of growing up wanting to be like women because there are no men around for them to take example from. Too many of our boys take on the characteristics of women, because the woman is the dominant factor in their

lives. Much of the homosexuality that we see in our streets today
has been developed, among other things, because of the lack of
male images. Among girls, too, homosexuality is on the rise for
various reasons. The growing trend must be halted.

Now, with respect to morals: The church must give moral
guidelines to young people that they might have a Christian interpretation about sex. Sex is the big bugaboo of youth; they
want to know "what to do about sex." Today young people con-
tinually face the physical appeal of sex in an open and frank
society. In this sex-charged atmosphere where the emphasis is on
sexuality everywhere, we of the church have to emphasize the
spiritual dimensions of sex.

God has provided the sex experience for the sake of physically
communicating love that cannot be put into any other form of
expression. As such it is God given. Sex is not of the devil. Sex
is not evil. Sex is not sinful. It is of God. The existence of life
depends upon it. Sex is of God, and it is the highest form of
human love. Therefore, it is to be experienced and used on the
highest plane of human contact. But it does not belong in the
gutter or in the back alley as it is put today, and used and de-
based as something nasty or impure. Rather, sex to fulfill its God-
given purpose is to be linked to the highest expression of human
love and to the creation of the family and to the development
of the home! In this context it becomes not nasty or impure, but
beautiful and biologically productive as essential for the maintaining of the human race.

We must, therefore, help our young people to regard the sex
act on the highest possible marital plane and not as something
to be experimented with in the back seat of a car, or at an out-
door movie, or at some hidden rendezvous. I know it will be hard
for young people to adhere to this view of sex. A young boy or
girl in the late teens is biologically at a peak in vitality and
passions. Modern drugs have removed much of the fear of
venereal disease, and enlightenment on birth control and the availability of pharmaceuticals have removed much of the fear of
pregnancy. Fear of "what could happen" is no longer of con-
sequence in restraining boys and girls, as when we adults grew
up. But actually, fear has always been a poor reason for restraining young couples. Fear did not work in the past, and fear

will not work in the future. Those of us in the older generation did what we wanted to do anyway, in spite of fear of what might happen. Rather than, therefore, to depend on fear, we must help teenagers to develop personal, moral, and religious convictions, born out of a religious faith and the desire to do what is best and right. We must not only tell our children what is morally right to do, but we must also strive to give to them the strength to do what is morally right. Our boys and our girls must find the inner ability to practice restraint and control until they can be as sure as they can be that their expressions of love are not a folly, but have a lasting quality pointed toward the development of Christian homes.

Let our young girls guard their virginity with all possible diligence—and our young boys gain strength to hold up the morals of the race. May the young of the Black race be purer and do better than was done by us of the older generation, and through self-discipline may they establish new standards of godly behavior.

May our young Black people be able to rise to the pinnacle of God's purest mountain and thereby set a new example for a decaying Western world. In so doing we may save the life and the soul of a decadent White man who does not realize it but who is on the way to becoming a dying race.

Finally, let us encourage our youth to have faith in themselves and to help them to develop their latent, but great, inner possibilities and potentials.

There is an idealism in young Black kids that has never at all been realized. White kids have gotten where they wanted to go, and now they want to throw everything away. But Black children, for the most part, have not had anything worthwhile materially to throw away. The great opportunities of life have been held back from them. There is an idealism in our children to be somebody and to accomplish something. This spirit of idealism is in the bosom of almost every Black child I know. Black kids on the whole do not want to get involved in gang war or to destroy. They are rather trying to prove the only way they know that they are somebody. They want to be recognized. They want something of their own. Therefore, they talk about protecting "their turf." But the fact is, they *are* somebody! They should be recognized. We must help them to be recognized.

Recently, one of my happiest evenings was spent when, at a large Philadelphia hotel, I attended a banquet given by a group of young Black youth from many sections of North Philadelphia who named themselves the "Congressional Soul Gents." As I looked at these fine young people, at the boys dressed handsomely in their tuxedos and the girls dressed beautifully in their gowns, I saw in them the idealism and insight of the Black youth of America. The boys stood tall and they were handsome, and the girls were Black beauties. In that setting they were saying to themselves and to all of us adults: "We are somebody. All we want is someone to help us to prove what we can be and do." It was difficult for me to make that banquet, but I made it and I am glad I did. For there is where I belonged. I got more joy being at the banquet of the Congressional Soul Gents that night, than last year when I attended a dinner in the White House. There are thousands and thousands of youth like these who want to prove what they can be and do.

The church must respond to the needs of our children and encourage them to believe in themselves and to let them know that "we care!" As Christians and as a church, through our daily efforts and through our programs we have to encourage our youth to have faith in themselves—and to let them know we care. If we don't care about our own Black children and don't help them, no one else will.

As we face these complicated problems of morality, marriage life, encouragement of the Black youth, and the unifying of the home, we have many allies to help us. We have scientific research and psychologists who continue to give us new insights into the human mind and human personality. But the greatest ally that we have to help us is still the word of God, the work of the church, and the influencing power of the Lord Jesus Christ in the lives of the people. For the main problems of love, marriage, sex, and the home still demand a Christian answer, Christian strength, and Christian resolve and prayer.

It is my hope that we shall leave the church today with some Christian answers to these dire and urgent problems, with a new strength and with a new resolve. May our lives be just a little bit better than they were before we came to church today. And may we be willing, each in his or her own way, to help, however best we can, to halt the moral decay in our communities, so we might know that "in spite of it all," there is still hope, with God's help, for the nation, for the race, and for the world. For there is hope and God is not dead. He still lives!

The World-Saving Power of the Bible
A SERMON

"The law of the Lord is perfect,
  reviving the soul;
the commandment of the Lord is pure,
  making wise the simple;
the testimony of the Lord is sure,
  rejoicing the heart;
the precepts of the Lord are right,
  enlightening the eyes. . . ."
  —*Psalm 19:7-8*

Of all the inspirational manuscripts and books written since the beginning of civilization, none can compare or even come near equalizing the importance or the power or the transforming influence of the Word of God. Of all the mountains of essays and stories and histories that have been written by man, nothing that man has written of himself comes near in importance, in meaning, and in power to the Bible, the Word of God. The Bible has been the greatest single force in the world to counsel and to inspire men to move forward and to act courageously and to change their ways of living. Nothing has inspired men to higher, clearer, nobler, cleaner, and more service-directed ways of life than the Bible. The great men who have made their contributions to the development of brotherhood and understanding and who have pointed the way to progress for our world have all had an inexpressible passion for the Word of God.

Though Joshua was engaged for most of his life in leading men to bloody battle, we are told that the Books of Moses, the Pentateuch, the Word of God as he knew it then, never departed from his mouth. He meditated on it day and night. Job, whose

77

example in the midst of trouble has inspired us through the ages to wait on God until a change for the better comes, esteemed the Word of God more than his necessary food. Ezekiel walked and talked about God's word so much that he dreamed he saw himself literally chewing, digesting, and assimilating the manuscripts of God's Word. We are told that the Bible was John Bunyan's sole companion for years. Everywhere he went, he had his Bible with him, and its influence can be read in every line of *Pilgrim's Progress*. It is said that Spurgeon and Moody, who preached thousands away from the door of hell and who made the world move toward the cross of Jesus, wore out two or three Bibles a year.

The power of the preaching of Billy Graham is in his Bible teaching. Wherever you see Billy preaching, you see the Bible in his hand. All through the Psalms the poet is singing about and writing about his inexpressible love for the Word of God. At one point his heart is so overflowing that he exclaims, "How I love thy word, O God!" and in the tenth verse of the Nineteenth Psalm, in speaking of the Word of God, he says:

> More to be desired are they than gold,
> even much fine gold;
> sweeter also than honey
> and drippings of the honeycomb.

Men who love the Bible get power from on high. Abe Lincoln loved the Bible and read it and the Bible came into his life and fused his soul, and he had power from on high. Frederick Douglass believed in God's Word, and he had power from on high. George Washington Carver loved the Bible, read in it, thought about it, prayed about it, and he had power from on high. Albert Schweitzer loved the Bible, and he had power from on high. Martin Luther King loved the Bible, was guided by the Bible; his life was infused with the Bible, and he had power from on high.

Yes, in the lives of great men, ancient and current, whose deeds have stirred history, the Word of God was ever at the center of their lives. In all that they did they were guided by the Word of God. They read God's Word, they kept their ears tuned to heaven to hear what God had to say, letting God direct them in their lives.

Today, though, the love of the Bible is far from the case. For in this day the Bible does not have a preeminent place in most of our lives. It is the most unread, untended, unfollowed book in the world, in spite of its volumes of publication. In it we have answers to every problem, worldly and personal, but we do not know it because we do not read it. All over the world our ignorance of the Bible is lamentable. We can talk to our young educated men and women about anything, intellectually, except the Bible. They know about everything else except the Bible, and it is lamentable. They are at home with you when you talk with them about *Ivanhoe* and about Chaucer, about the *Iliad* and the *Odyssey,* about Shakespeare and the essays of Bacon and Emerson, or the books of our contemporary authors. They can talk with you intelligently about Jean Paul Sartre or James Baldwin, but as soon as you mention the Bible, they turn away. They are not interested in that. It is not real enough to them, not exciting enough—dry and uninteresting, they say.

But the Bible is never dry and uninteresting. From a purely literary point of view, it is the best book that ever came from the press. Show me history more ancient than "In the beginning God created the heavens and the earth." Show me biography more interesting than the lives of Jacob, Joseph, and Daniel; love stories more charming than the Book of Ruth; poetry more inspiring than the Psalms of David and the Songs of Solomon; rhetoric more sublime than the writings of Isaiah; logic more convincing than the epistles of Paul; eloquence more uplifting than the words of Him who spake as man never spake; geology more wonderful than that of the splintered, smoking, fiery crest of Sinai; zoology more puzzling than that which Daniel demonstrated in the lion's den; chemical problems more perplexing than that of the Hebrew boys cast into the fiery furnace; botanical specimens more fascinating than the Rose of Sharon and the Lily of the Valley. Dry and uninteresting? Oh, what can be more filled with vibrancy, power, excitement, and passion than the Word of God! If only we could turn the world to the Word of God, for it is the Word of God that has the answers to the terrifying problems of mankind.

We want a law to live by. "The law of the Lord is perfect, converting the soul." We want a testimony that is sure. "The testimony of the Lord is sure, making wise the simple." We want statutes to abide by that are right. "The statutes of the Lord are right, rejoicing the heart." We are looking for a commandment that will point us in the right direction. "The commandment of the Lord is pure, enlightening the eyes" (see Psalm 19, KJV). Oh, that we might stop in this hurly-burly age and get a new grip on the Word of God! For the Word of God is sure. There is nothing else you can depend on, but you can depend on the Word of God.

And when New York City is no more, when Philadelphia is no more, when you and I are no more, the Word of God will still be here, for the Word of God is sure. When the stars shall be extinguished like sparks from a blacksmith's anvil, the Word of God will still be here. When this old earth shall lie wrecked like a smashed automobile on the highway to eternity, the Word of God will still be here. For God has declared, "The grass withers, the flower fades, but the word of our God shall stand for ever" (Isaiah 40:8).

So let us here in this day take hold of the Word of God. In this coming week let us go back to our homes and dust off our Bibles and spend a few minutes with the Word of God. Turn to the Psalms and read a few lines. Give God a chance in your life. Take a little time with God's Word. Read it, believe it, then trust your life to it. It will fill your life with happiness, for the only way to be happy is to get God's Word in you. "The statutes of the Lord are right, rejoicing the heart." It will not only give you happiness here, but it will give you happiness that will last forever. People everywhere are looking for happiness. Some go to the valleys of California or to Florida looking for happiness. Some take steamers to Italy and travel to the Bay of Naples looking for happiness. Some climb to the top of mountain peaks. Some drink, some wear fine gowns, some frequent nightclubs and dances and parties, looking for happiness. Some try to accumulate money thinking it will bring them happiness; some acquire property, looking for happiness. Some use dope or LSD, looking vainly for happiness. You won't find it in any of these ways. But if you want to find that elusive bluebird of happiness, it can be found, if you will get the Word of God in your heart and let it have a permanent place in your life. You will be happy in your home, happy on the streets, happy at your work, happy wherever you go. "The statutes of the Lord are right, rejoicing the heart." And the Word of God can change the directions of the lives of people in turmoil anywhere.

A few years ago when I came to my present church in Philadelphia, I was walking along the street to view the parish area where I was to minister. I saw five boys on the corner with nowhere to go. I went back to my church and took an old basketball that I had brought with me all the way from West Virginia, and I took it to where the boys were and threw the ball to one of them. He dropped it. The five boys and I went to an old church building that had been converted into a gymnasium, and all day long we played basketball together. I found that of these five boys, most of them had already dropped out of school. Three of them already had police records. All of them had hopelessness in their hearts and anger in their minds; they all felt that the world had closed them out. Not one of them belonged to a church. Not one of them belonged to a Sunday school. I invited these boys to Sunday school the next morning, and all five of them came. They stayed for church. Later I baptized all five of those boys.

A few years ago we analyzed what had happened to some of the boys and girls who had come to the community programs of our church. This is what had happened to those five boys, all of whom had zero records as far as the community was concerned. One had become a supervisor with the Philadelphia Gas Works. Another had become an executive with OIC. The third boy was a special agent in the narcotics squad in Washington, D.C. The fourth boy was a professional basketball player, making three times as much playing basketball as I was making preaching. The fifth boy became the first Phi Beta Kappa to graduate from Howard University. He came back to Philadelphia, graduated near the top of his class at Temple Medical School, and is now an officer in my church. The Word of God can change the lives of boys and girls and men and women. The Word of God can change the direction of lives. The church still has the message of salvation. The church still has the message to save boys and girls and men and women from the damnation of hate and frustration on earth now. The Word of God has power to change lives.

And the Word of God will do something more. It will transform your whole body and change your whole life. You look like the person with whom you associate. Association begets assimilation. This is the unchangeable law of nature and God; so then get to know Jesus and you will begin to look like him. You will begin to look like him in your face and in your eyes. For when a man becomes converted, he looks different. He acts different. He walks different. He *is* different. My grandmother used to say to me, "I looked at my hands and my hands looked new. I looked at my feet and they looked so too." I now understand the Word of God changes every part of a man who decides to live for Jesus.

So, I appeal to you this day. Let the Word of God have a main place in your life. Hold the Bible in your heart. Whatever others say, it is the hope of the world. Keep the Word of God in your heart and you shall find your joy, you shall find your freedom, you shall find your happiness, you shall find your life.

Let us pray:

Eternal God, have mercy upon us and bless us to thy purpose and thy calls and may the Word of God have a preeminent place in our hearts, filling our lives.

Amen.

A New American Alliance

Speech given at the 8th annual OIC convocation, Washington, D.C.

The genius of America has been in the nation's ability to solve our greatest problems: whether it be in the expansion of frontiers, the building of cities, or putting a man on the moon. In the past there has been no problem too great for America to solve.

Today America is faced with one of her greatest challenges. We are faced with the need to bring forty million fellow Americans into the mainstream of the benefits of the American way of life and the free enterprise system. These forty million citizens represent every section and every color in the nation. They are all living beneath or just above the poverty line, and although things are getting better for the rest of America, things are getting worse for them. For the sake of America the problem of providing for the needs of the poor, the unemployed, and the underemployed must be solved, or else it will grow and grow until it pulls the whole nation under.

By the year 2000, one-half of all the jobs being done now in our country will not even exist. New jobs will have taken their places. People must be trained and retrained to do these new jobs as the old ones fade away. If we do not prepare our people on a massive scale with new manpower training and new job opportunities, the results to the nation will be devastating. OIC wants to help do that job.

If we do not significantly begin to solve the problem now, by the year 2000, taking just the Black population alone, one out of every two will have to be subsidized by some form of relief, costing the nation, at today's cost, $50 billion in welfare; and for the whole nation the cost could well exceed $200 billion. This condition will lead to national bankruptcy and domestic chaos. We must deal with the situation now when it is still at proportions that can be handled.

Therefore, for the good of the nation, it is time for a new American alliance to deal with the situation at hand—a new American alliance linking industry and business with the poor. Therefore, it will be OIC's goal in the next few years to mobilize ten thousand businesses and companies in America behind the work of OIC in the greatest pulling together of American enterprise behind the efforts of our needy, in the history of this nation, to solve our manpower-training needs. We will want businesses, large and small, to know that in OIC they have an ally in progress.

Let industry and business create the jobs and let OIC recruit and train in attitudes and skills for the jobs, thereby creating the power to produce more, to buy more, and thus to help make the wheel of America's prosperity go round and round. In this new American alliance we will help each other: American industry and the people.

Let us visit every business, every company, every factory, and every plant, in every city where OICs are established, and let there be ten thousand businesses helping with jobs and supporting the work of OIC across America. This new alliance between industry and the poor had better work, because our fates are tied together. If it doesn't work, one day we will all go out of business.

And let all companies and businesses that work with OIC do it from a commitment, rather than from paternalism. If you say you are with OIC and the poor, I ask you to be with us all the way. Be with us in the employment of our people. Be with us in the upgrading of minority workers. Be with us in seeing that justice is done for the Black and the Brown workers, wherever they are employed with equal opportunity. We don't need friends with us who kiss us on the cheek on one side and knock us in the head on the other side.

If this new American alliance between industry and the poor is going to work, it will have to be out of a commitment to Americanize American industry from the bottom to the top, and not because some government officials or congressmen or organizations or individuals are putting the pressure behind you. Let it be known to those who help us that we will help them; and to those who do not help us, that we will not help them. And the greatest help that we can offer or withhold is our purchasing power. Industry wants it and respects it. We are "getting ourselves together" all over the nation. Whereas before we were blind, now we see.

Let there be a new alliance between government and the nation's underprivileged. Make no mistake about it, the government cannot solve the problems of the underprivileged alone. Government is too tied up in the conditions that create the problems. But OIC can help the government to solve the problem if the government will help OIC and work with OIC to get the job done.

Let the federal government provide support for OIC to demonstrate in one hundred cities, on a significant scale, our unique capabilities. As the federal government has used Lockheed in a special way for its war needs, let the government now use OIC in a special way in a new offensive against welfare, unemployment, and depression.

OIC does not expect, nor does it want, to do all the manpower training in America. To assume such a thing would be foolish and unthinkable, but we do want the opportunity, in a major way, to help our brothers and sisters in the country, in the concentrated communities of America, in the rural areas, and on the plantations and reservations, *where other conventional federal manpower-training programs just have not reached.*

OIC is not just a manpower program; it is much more than that. OIC is designed to help the whole man. OIC does not just train people for jobs; OIC trains people for *life.* OIC is interested in motivating people for total self-improvement: with skills, with attitudes, and with respect for themselves and their fellowmen.

OIC wants to train one hundred thousand men and women a year for jobs that exist by 1973 and to train one million men and women into productive jobs by the end of this decade. It will require a minimum of $100 million a year to reach our goal, at a cost four times lower than the cost of any federal training program in America today. And the payoff from OIC's efforts will be phenomenal. It will mean $30 billion in new incomes for America and $10 billion saved in relief checks. Since most of this new income will be recycled five times in purchasing power in a city, it could mean as much as $150 billion added to the national gross product. Our efforts could begin to stem the tide of welfarism in America.

So then, let the government provide help to us through a new manpower bill that will soon be coming before the Congress that must be passed for the good of the nation, *with special funds provided for OIC in that bill,* SOMEHOW.

But let the government remember that OIC does not need yo-yo funds, with a string to manipulate up or down, or zigzag, or around. We want federal administrators to help us, but not to hinder us. OIC does not need anyone to tell us how to do the job; we just need the resources to be able to do it for ourselves. This is revenue sharing at the best, for we are sharing the revenues of the government with a program of the people, who, through self-help, are striving to help themselves to put their heads up and their shoulders back and to stand upon their feet. And as far as our management capability is concerned, I am proud to say that we will have General Electric and General Motors and the Chase Manhattan Bank and Arthur B. Little Company, and many others of ability and resource standing by our side helping us to develop our management capability as we go along.

Finally, let us make a new American alliance between the peoples of America. We have been at each other's throats long enough. It is time we came out of our ethnic and racial corners and decided to help build America together. The day for racial animosity and racial hatred is over. We have created a stalemate between our people that has only served to divide us further. America does not need to be divided anymore. America needs to be united; because if the ship goes down, we will all go down together, with it.

So we need a new American alliance of the American people including us all. I believe in Black Power, I helped make Black Power in America, I am a part of Black Power, and I am proud of it; but the time has come to knock down the walls between us and to take Black Power and White Power and Brown Power and put them together to build AMERICAN POWER that we might all walk up the road of American opportunities—together.

It is a new American alliance that I ask for today: of business with the poor, of government with the underprivileged, of Black and Brown and Red and White—and, together, we shall build a greater nation of true prosperity and benefits for us all.

Right on!

3
BLACK
ECONOMIC
DEVELOPMENT

I firmly believe that Black people must be integrated into the mainstream of American life. Black economic development has to be accomplished in terms of integration! There is no such thing as Black capitalism! There is no such thing as Black capital!

The economy in this country is tied into everything, everybody, and everything that happens. We can't have one economic system for the White man and another for the Black man. There must be one economic system and that has to be for everyone. Within that system Black people can develop their own business enterprises, just as the White population and various specific ethnic groups have often done over the years.

What the Black man is saying is that he must develop enterprises which are not just for Black people—just as White enterprises haven't been just for Whites. All over the country Black people buy Ford automobiles sold by Whites. All over the country Black people eat Kellogg's corn flakes produced in a factory owned and operated by Whites. The Black man, like his White brother, must be able to produce commodities that can be dispensed in the free markets of the country and the free markets of the world. He must be able to compete as an integral part of the system of free enterprise. The problem has been that the Black man hasn't even been in a competitive position; he hasn't even seen the side door of free enterprise so as to know what it involves.

His paramount need is to get inside the door in terms of management, in terms of knowing what the economic structure is, in terms of development and control of capital. Then he will be able to move step by step through the process of building economic strength. In the final analysis the country, in fact the world, is run on money. Although *people* run on spirit, the nation is run on money, enterprise is developed on money, communities are built on money. Communities are built to help the people utilize money.

Unfortunately, Blacks have not had the financial capital that they have needed to develop enterprises. They have always been on the consuming instead of the producing end. If you take all the businesses owned by the Blacks in America today, the total would comprise less than one-half of 1 percent of the business in the country. If all of the Black businesses were combined, their corporate net value would barely exceed one billion dollars. You can ride hundreds of miles before you find a single motel owned by a Black man today, or by a Black group or even by a group in which a Black man is a part. You can see hundreds of factories while traveling thousands of miles, and you will be hard put to find a single factory which is owned or controlled by Blacks or that would even have a Black man on the board. It is obvious; the Black man has been on the outside of the production and ownership of American industry. This is true although his people make up approximately 12 to 13 percent of the population in the United States today, and by the year 2000 this figure will be from 16 to 20 percent. In the year 2000, it is estimated

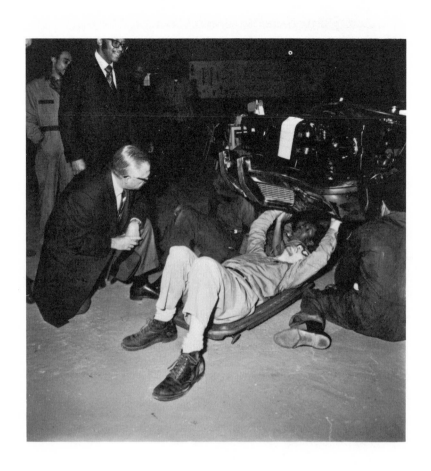

that there will be 300 million people in America and these will include 60 million Blacks. Right now is the time when we have to move into Black ownership of businesses with the realization that we have to pay as we go.

Many of the Black businesses will not succeed, just as many of the White businesses have not succeeded. The majority of businesses fail, and many that continue to exist yield only minimal profit, really operating on a shoestring. However, we must accept the risk of failure if we are going to have the hope of success.

Black people are going to have to develop skills in merchandising. They need to develop the ability in sales management. Most of the money made in America is made on the sales market. If, for example, one is to realize a million dollars a year, one must make several big sales of large commodities in the excess of a million dollars. Such are the facts of life in the business community. A man who sells ten computers can make ten million dollars; a real estate man who sells two big office buildings can make a million dollars; a man who sells a ship can make four million dollars from the sale. However, a man must have adequate knowledge about merchandise; he must have developed a productive ability; and he must be able to conclude the sale. This achievement requires the development of a class of Blacks who are oriented in terms of management, ownership, and sales.

At the present time there are a few Blacks who represent what we call the "top Black," and many times they do not relate to the rest of the Blacks but seek to become White. As a result, almost all of the big mass of Blacks remain in a disadvantaged state, living on their weekly or monthly wages. They are able to save very little. They comprise the big mass of Blacks in this country. They are locked in ghettos and are unable to get out. They don't have the money, the jobs, or the skills.

On the contrary, there are stories of White men who came to America from someplace else, or those who have been raised in this country who have become economically secure because they have developed businesses and sales. We are going to have to develop in this country parallel examples from the Black community. I say this not just to the Black community, but to the whole community, because we can't have an economy with only the Blacks or an economy with only the Whites. We must have a world economy and the Black man must be integrated into that economy. The modern world leans toward the integration of the Black man in the economy of all men.

Progress Plaza (our Black owned and operated shopping center in Philadelphia) and other economic ventures are cases in point. All of these programs are founded on this philosophy which I mentioned above.

American industry could learn a great deal from Mark Morton, Vice President of the General Electric Corporation about how to help minorities get successful enterprises going. He and his company were vital in the initiation of the Progress Avionics Enterprise which is located in Philadelphia and which has developed into one of the truly great success stories of minority enterprises in America.

To be truly emancipated, a man must be emancipated economically as well as psychologically and physically. He must be emancipated in his pocketbook. If a man thinks he is mentally and socially emancipated, but if he doesn't have any money, he fools himself. He has false, unrealistic fixations. If he can't be made to see the real anymore, he can be reenslaved. So in my understanding of emancipation, I believe a man should have an economic emancipation and that he should have it abundantly. "Ask, and it will be given you; seek and you will find; knock, and it will be opened to you" (Matthew 7:7).

Another factor in this approach to economic liberation is that we have to utilize the resources we have in order to be economically emancipated. Before we started the OIC, we began a program that would generate capital for Blacks so that

they could develop businesses, enterprises, and housing programs of their own. I looked in the Bible one Saturday night and I was reading about the feeding of the five thousand (Mark 6:34-44). If Jesus himself could multiply a few loaves and fishes and feed five thousand people and have a few loaves left over, even that supernatural act would not have been as remarkable as the miracle of sharing that I believe really happened that day. The significant thing is that Jesus challenged the people to share what they had. Everybody—every man and every child and every woman—responded by doing just that. The miracle was the result of sharing. For the common good of all, they shared. Out of this sharing there was more than enough food for all. Jesus performed a miracle in getting the people to share what they had.

So I went to my church and after preaching a sermon on gathering the fragments of life, I asked fifty members to invest ten dollars a month. The money could be used in two ways, one for nonprofit purposes in which there would be no immediate return, such as to build health facilities, to finance nonprofit housing developments, to develop educational scholarship funds, and to provide care for the sick and the infirm. The other portion would go into a profit venture. Initially not fifty, but two hundred people responded. Their response formed the base for the 10-36 Plan. The idea was not that they would receive but that their children and their children's children would receive. This plan provides the basis of opportunity for those who are coming after us. Once a person puts his money in the pot, he knows it will come back; it will come back when he is sick or when he is old; it will come back in benefits to his heirs, his assignees, his children, his grandchildren, his great grandchildren, or to those friends who don't have children.

I told the people that many others would benefit from the sacrifices that they made. Utimately, of course, they themselves would get benefits, once the ventures became profitable. Profit sharing encouraged them. Later they were to put their dividends back into the investment to expand the businesses. In 10-36 the common man was getting a part of the action while at the same time helping to build his community!

This activity is what I call the reverse syndrome of welfare. Instead of people continuing to be a drain on society, they were building up a reverse and giving input to persons and to the total community. I was trying to turn welfare around to become something that is positive. From programs and funds such as this the people would be able to help themselves. Through "reversal of welfare" the church and church people could, by their own resources, develop themselves and provide assistance by "helping themselves!" The Rockefellers have done similarly for the welfare of their family. They have bought a lot of apartment buildings in New York, which produce rental income to support their families. Their descendants should never have to work to earn money for themselves. They are living off the wealth of their families by the wise investments of their forebears. Many other large, wealthy families, like the Fords and Mellons, are also living off the fruits of their forebears.

This is what I am trying to do with meager funds that are available by each sharing what he has. In this way the benefits from the immediate investment will come back a hundred years from now, perhaps even a thousand years from now.

Here we were with two hundred people pooling their money to build a million-dollar apartment complex, the first built by Blacks in Philadelphia. Soon we had some six hundred people participating in the program, and we built a two-million-dollar shopping center—the first shopping center built by Blacks in America, perhaps the largest in the world built by Blacks. Then we opened the plan to five thousand people and as a result we built the first and largest aerospace company in the world owned by Blacks. Later we opened supermarkets where the Whites and the Blacks shopped together. We sought to develop a chain so that our food markets would be throughout Philadelphia and one day throughout America.

In this way we began to generate new capital. We began to buy office buildings. We worked the income from some of these into a charitable trust so that the income ultimately can improve education and provide scholarships. I call this money "Community Capital."

This effort began to move like a snowball so that by the time the Securities and Exchange Commission registered the "10-36 Plan" we could claim that this was the first time in history that stock issues which were both nonprofit and profit in nature had ever been registered by the federal government. Here is the plan:

Twenty thousand issues were placed on sale initially all over the country. We will have twenty thousand people giving ten dollars per month for thirty-six months. Our plan is to add up to as many as a half million shareholders all over the country, so that the kind of programs we developed in Philadelphia can be developed in up to one hundred cities.

The plan is for Blacks, Browns, Reds, and Whites. Everything I do is for all. I initiate the programs as a Black man with Black leadership but Whites can participate in anything I do, because I don't believe in a Black world or a White world. I believe in one world and in one America. I think Blacks must initiate; Blacks must lead in the ventures I conceive. I think that for long enough Whites have led Blacks in everything they have done. Now it is time for Black leadership, Black confidence, and the Black's turn, so that we can balance the system. But the White investors are welcome.

I particularly want church people to participate in the efforts to uplift the community as well as themselves. In this way we can change the mentality of Blacks from the "hand out" to the "put in" philosophy.

We have a training program for everything we do. People will be trained in what this plan is all about, wherever we have OIC and other institutional programs. In this way the people can be informed about this type of program and the benefits from it. This type of program can be used to build so much in our communities: shopping centers, housing developments, factories, investment houses, banks, and most of all, pride in ownership, and confidence.

The "10-36 Plan" is community ownership at its purest and at its best. Every person feels that he has a part, and he has! The ten dollars a month for thirty-six months yields $360, of which $160 goes to a nonprofit charitable trust. The other $200 goes to progress. The arrow pointing up, which is the "10-36" symbol, is the kind of direction I'm hoping that we can take—upward. This is Black economic development. I want to see 10-36 spread community by community across America. Anywhere a Black man goes in America, I want him to have strength because the 10-36 Plan is behind him; and whenever a Black child is seen, I want him to be respected because his parents are building something.

Another aspect of Black economic development is what I call AAE (Adult Armchair Education). This is a very interesting program on consumer education. I got the name when I was in a parsonage of a Baptist church in Springfield, Massachusetts. I was sitting in a big chair and the pastor was talking with me about a big problem that his people were facing. They were living in a community and being cheated by people who kept them in debt. At the same time they did not know how to stretch their money.

I decided then that it would be necessary to develop home-to-home group meetings in small units to deal with this problem, and that it should be a relaxed kind of situation so that the men could come with no ties on and the women without a lot of dressy clothes. This would be a place where people could sit and talk about their mutual problems. Therefore, it had to be a setting where people could learn literacy: reading, writing, and arithmetic. It would have to be called—as in the OIC—Communication Skills and Computational Arts, so that people wouldn't be embarrassed at studying elementary subjects in their adult lives.

"Communication Skills," of course, refers to English in-

struction, and "Computational Arts" refers to arithmetic or mathematics. However, the main focus would be on consumer education so that people could learn how to spend and use their money, how to balance whatever little budget they had; how to make more money, and in the process how to tell more about the items they purchased (how to tell fresh chicken from that which is spoiled, how to read the markings on bread wrappers so as not to get stale loaves, how to understand the markings on cans of tuna or other products that are intended to protect the consumer). This training had to be done in a network so that it wouldn't reach only a few but many.

In this program of Adult Armchair Education (AAE), consumer education is built around the way people are being cheated by stores in the communities. This happens in big and little stores wherever foodstuff is sold. For example, the large supermarkets will take the leftovers from the suburban areas where the food has become old and overripe, and they shine it off and square it up so that it looks good and ship it down to the Black community. The AAE program will contribute to public health by helping people to know what they are getting (whether it's fresh fruit) and also whether they are getting what they are paying for.

Blacks have to pay 10 percent more just to live in the ghettos. When corn is 27 cents in the suburbs, it is often 30 cents in the ghetto. Blacks have to pay 10 percent more, and often more than that, for rent for quarters comparable to those for Whites, 10 percent more for insurance (when they can get it at all), and even 10 percent more for funerals— caskets are often 10 percent higher in price. Consequently, an average Black family with an income of $7,000 pays $700 in overcharges and higher prices. Considering that one of every four Black families lives in the ghetto in America, Black families are being exploited in an amount of one billion dollars. Not only this, Blacks even die 10 percent faster, partly because pollution is so much worse in the slums than in the suburbs. AAE helps people to cope with these problems. Scales in many markets are adjusted to cheat the people. Many people do not realize that weights have to be inspected and that there should be an inspection notice indicating that the weights have been inspected. The AAE program reminds the people that the stores must be inspected and that at least a minimal standard of sanitation should prevail. AAE teaches people how to buy and what to buy. This kind of training is what we call consumer education.

This education was extended to include knowledge about living in houses, about public and private landlords. People are informed of the need for property inspections, their responsibilities as tenants as well as the responsibilities of the landlords. The landlord has rights, too, and tenants have to learn that a landlord can't be expected to rent a property after a tenant destroys everything that makes it a home. So this problem is a two-sided affair. Not everything is a problem of the landlord; some things are problems of the tenant. The tenant should know what the responsibility of each is. The landlord must make a profit, we understand that, but it cannot be the exorbitant profit that often is found where deteriorated urban apartments rent for much more than good apartments in the uncongested areas.

These programs became an exciting part of the development of the whole OIC program. We were able to pull support from the total religious community. In Philadelphia we were able to draw a considerable amount of support from the Catholic leadership as well as from Protestant churches of all denominations. Many of these churches sponsored armchair groups. In the Jewish community, many groups have formed educational forums, providing an opportunity to talk with Black leaders in their homes.

We have exchange meetings of individuals in Black communities and White communities, Jewish communities, and Catholic communities. People can begin to understand other communities and start working out the problems that usually affect everyone. It is my desire to see AAE groups increase

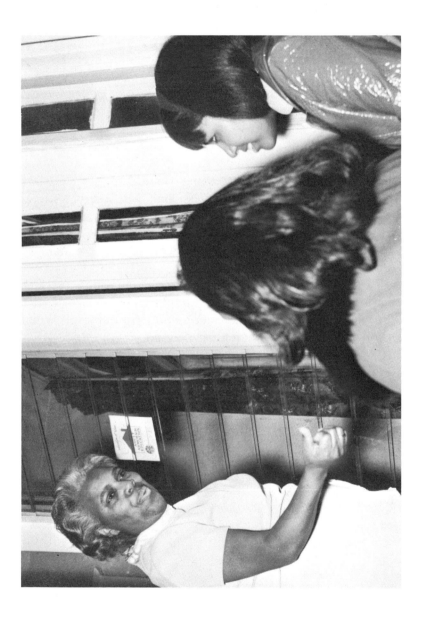

the community's role in the OIC network until they blanket America.

The AAE program is staffed usually by a small group of professionals who are trained in OIC techniques of the self-help concepts and who are from the local community. They are people who can relate to the problems of the community. They are supplemented by the use of White and Black professional leadership, but we use Black leaders, minority leaders, and Mexican Americans, in our homes for the most part. There are Whites who understand the dignity of the Black people and also realize that being White isn't always being right. The leaders, lay or professional, work very well together. Our experience has proven that Blacks and Whites can work together with common respect. This, too, is what I am working for. I am trying to liberate the White man as well as the Black man.

Throughout the program of consumer education the emphasis is on human relations. It is the best way we have found to place instructional relations on a really fruitful level. When people are in a common setting, they are able to discuss human problems that affect everyone. That is the curriculum.

I'm doing these things to Americanize America. I see these projects as an extension of my ministry because I'm trying to prove that God is no respecter of persons and that God is father of us all. Instead of doing it all in the church, we are doing some of it in the homes, because the home is still the most important unit in the development of society.

A Land of Glory and of Shame
A SERMON

"If my people who are called by my name humble themselves, and pray and seek my face, and turn from their wicked ways, then I will hear from heaven, and will forgive their sin and heal their land."
—2 Chronicles 7:14

Never in the history of mankind has a nation possessed the glory of America. It is as though the hand of God were above us, providing resources, possessions, and accumulations of blessings to compare with the days of fabled Aladdin. America is rich and blessed with incomparable natural glories. No land in the world possesses such wealth of natural resources and climatic conditions so favorable for the needs and benefits of its people.

America is blessed with geographic glories. Isolated by expansions of oceans from the rest of a world torn by ageless conflicts, America geographically stands alone; separated by great oceans; geographically apart, kept free from the ravages, the calamities, and the tragedies of destructive war.

America is blessed with political glories. Ours is a republic that has weathered the vicissitudes of disagreements among our peoples; we have a form of government and system that supersedes and excels anything ever devised and tested to govern men anywhere. In spite of its inadequacies, our American political system with its checks and balances, is still the finest to be found in the world.

America is blessed with economic glory. The gross national produce of this nation exceeds one trillion dollars. Our people are better off by far, economically, than any other people who have lived in the history of the world: and, in spite of the recessions and inflations, the economic future of the nation is bright.

America is blessed with ethnic glory. We are the melting pot of the world. Here, all nationalities, races, and colors have converged to form a global accumulation of humanity never before so imperially diversified in color and kind and thought. It is here that the experiment of "One World" is being carried on in a very real way. Here, in America today, whether men of different nationalities, races, and colors can live together is being tested. If we can make "One World" work here, then it can work anywhere.

America is blessed with religious glory. In this nation men are free to worship and serve God according to the dictates of their consciences, as each of us in his own way feels best. Whether a man believes in the cross or the crescent, in the star of Judah or the star of Bethlehem, or if he claims no faith at all, he is free to worship and to serve God as he pleases.

But, though America is a land of glories, unfortunately, too, America is a land of shame. Nowhere is there so much plenty, yet so much sorrow. Nowhere do men have so much, and yet have so little. Nowhere is there so much freedom, and yet so much bondage. Nowhere do men stand so tall, and yet stoop so low.

In a land of such plenty, still one-third of our population is ill housed, ill clothed, and ill fed. In a land of such plenty, still most of Black America, Chicano America, Indian America, Puerto Rican America, and Oriental America is shut out from the full benefits and opportunities of democracy and the free enterprise system. It costs the average Black man one hundred thousand dollars in a lifetime, just for being born Black, because of inequities in wages and restricted job opportunities.

The question has often been asked, "What does the Black man want?" The fact is that he wants no more than what the White man wants: an equal opportunity and an equal chance. If we were to make a sum total of losses to the Black population in America, for being born Black, because of inequities and discrimination, the sum total for thirty million Blacks would amount to $3 trillion, *just to cover the bill for the present generation.*

Several years ago America was "all shook up" over the question of reparations for Black men. Really, the idea was not as extreme as it sounded. For 246 years the Black man labored without a payday to build America. Actually, counting all, there is not sufficient money in the national treasury to make up in reparations or paybacks or in any other way for the cost of being born Black in America.

So in response to those who wonder whether it is fair to provide special opportunities for Blacks to move ahead in our society, the answer is an unequivocal "yes." For as the Black man has been kept back and held down by discrimination, it is time for the Black man to be helped up and pushed forward to better opportunities. As before we have been "discriminated against," it is only right that now the Black man should be "discriminated for." It will only be in this way that the books can ever be balanced.

Over and over again, we have heard it said that Black people are the *cause* of violence in the cities. But the fact is, the Black man is not the cause of violence; *rather* he is the *result* of violence: the violence of segregation and discrimination and humiliation. If America wants to get rid of violence in the concentrated communities of America, it can do so—not with riot guns or tear gas or tanks or beefed-up police forces, but by getting rid of the *roots* of violence, which are discrimination and segregation and humiliation. The Black man does not want very much—all the Black man wants is to be treated like an American and like a first-class human being. He wants nothing more, and in the future he will accept nothing less.

Those who believe that the cries for equality will somehow fade away should be reminded that there is a whole new generation coming along in our schools. Like a mighty wave, they are coming, Black and proud, and they will never accept the injustices of our generation. They are on the way. We might as well get ready for them now. *They are coming!* And they will be saying: "Either America will be America for everyone, or there will be no peace in America for anyone." *There is a need for a healing in the land,* as the text in 2 Chronicles 7:14 goes.

The problems facing America are deep and broad. In the case of housing, a great invisible wall separates most of the Black community from the White community. The Black man, by design, has been compressed into concentrated communities, surrounded by invisible walls of prejudice and discrimination that have kept him from spreading out and becoming a real part of the American dream. With all our laws and legislation and so-called good intent, still the fact remains that all kinds of devious means are used across the land to keep the suburbs White and to keep Blacks out.

Not long ago a young Black couple went to look at a house in a new housing development in an all-White section of Philadelphia. Going through the model house, they found no salesman there; but when they were about to leave, they opened the closet door in the hallway that led to the front door and found the salesman hiding inside. All kinds of tactics and tricks are used by lending institutions, banks, and mortgage houses (with some few exceptions) to keep the suburbs White and to keep Black people out.

The tragedy is that most of the White suburbs of America have been built over the last twenty years with funds insured by the federal government itself. In effect, the federal government has underwritten the development of segregated housing in the suburbs of America and has built superhighways to get to them. This is why I say: As the federal government has used its resources to foster segregation, then the federal government should use its resources now to promote integration. The invisible walls that keep men congested and compressed and concentrated in the hot, teeming, frustrated Black ghettos of America, *must* come down.

Yes, the problems are deep and broad. In job opportunities there is developing a situation of volcanic proportions. There are 400,000 veterans returned from the Vietnam war who are unemployed today. Of this number more than one-third are Black. These young men can be seen every day on the street corners of our big cities. They have returned from fighting for their country and there is nothing for them to do. They are disillusioned, they are idle, and they are mad. *These men have been trained to be the best killers in the world.* Either we find a way to employ their minds and their hands in useful work and meaningful pursuits, and help them to work their way constructively into society, or these men will turn on their community and on America, and they will cause disruptions and disorders so great that the riots in Watts will look like nothing in comparison.

Added to this condition is the fact that one out of every three Black men and women in America have incomes that fall beneath the poverty line. Millions of our people are on public assistance today, not because they want to be there but because there seems to be so little opportunity for them to earn a decent living with a decent job leading somewhere. Many say it is better to be on relief than to have some low-salaried dead-end job that only serves to perpetuate their poverty and frustration. The need for training and retraining programs on a massive scale in every neighborhood of every city in America is a priority need of

106

America. We must find a way to help a man to help himself, in order that with training and a skill he can do a job to provide for his family with dignity and with the belief that he is getting somewhere.

Other problems that beset the Black man, the Chicano, the Puerto Rican, and other minorities of color in large cities cover the full range of daily needs: public education, police harassment, rackets, graft, drugs, and politicians who use the problems as political footballs for their own selfish power and their own political advancement.

It is time now for the Christian church to speak, to make effective responses, to promote a new kind of Christian pragmatism. There is a pragmatic gospel that calls the church to new visions, new directions, and new action; a new Christian pragmatism that calls for not just milk and honey in heaven, but some ham and eggs on earth. A new Christian pragmatism that says: "Let us not just get men into heaven, but let us get heaven into men." A new Christian pragmatism that says: "Let us not just keep men out of hell, but let us get hell out of men." We need a new Christian pragmatism that will help men to build a better life on earth, for, if the church can help men to live on earth today as brothers, Black and White, then men can look to their peace in heaven, by and by. The Bible says to us: "Thus you will know them by their fruits" (Matthew 7:20).

Interestingly, a new religious revolution is welling up in the Black communities of America today, a revolution of this new pragmatism. Before, the White man has said to the Black man, "You take Jesus, and we'll take the world." But today, the Black man is saying, "We want Jesus, but we want some of the world, too." And out of the Black church of the concentrated community has emerged a program like OIC, the Opportunities Industrialization Center, a program of self-help, born out of faith, out of prayer, and out of a new kind of positive action.

Beginning in Philadelphia in 1964, in an old empty jailhouse, OIC, led by Black preachers and their congregations, has emerged as the most meaningful and exceptional manpower-training program, providing skills for the unemployed and the underemployed, in American history. The OIC program has spread by faith from that old jailhouse into one hundred cities across Amer-

107

ica, training tens of thousands of men and women every day, with new skills for new jobs that are leading them somewhere with a future. And the OIC has spread into Ghana, Nigeria, Ethiopia, Kenya, British Honduras, and the Dominican Republic—and it continues to spread.

The OIC says to a man, "You are like a balloon; it is not your color that makes you rise, but what you have inside of you." OIC says to a man, whether he be Black or Brown or Yellow or Red or poor Appalachian White: "Put your head up and your shoulders back and believe that you can make something of your life, and you will." OIC is in the business of motivating men to self-improvement.

OIC is not a government program. OIC is a people's program: a part of this new Christian pragmatism of men and women who do not believe that government has the answers to the problems of poverty and discrimination, because much of the government is a part of the problem itself. Therefore, we believe that we, the American people, must join our hands and our talents and our resources together to help solve the unemployment problems of America, with the full expectation that the government must back us up in our efforts.

But to accomplish what it is capable to do, OIC must be supported by the American people, with the help of government, but not run by the government; because if the government runs it, the government will ruin it.

If we continue to increase our capability, the impact of OIC could one day reach into every nook and corner of this nation and will help change the direction of America from a nation of welfare to a nation of opportunity and a good life for every man, woman, and child in the land.

And the American people must help!

Before this year is out, every American will be called upon to make a contribution to this OIC movement of self-help. Every individual, every business, every church, every foundation, and every agency will be called to do its part. Some will respond, and some will not, but all America will know this effort will go on. The train is on the track; those who want to get on board can get on if they want to, but if they don't, the train is going anyway. OIC must succeed. The survival of our children and our children's children is at stake, and in the final analysis the very survival of America is at stake. OIC must work!

If we are successful, and we hope to be, in our goal to train one million men and women into new skills and new jobs in the next decade, we shall add ten billion dollars in new purchasing power to America's economy. Considering the income multiplier at a minimum of five, based on the propensity to consume and the propensity to save, we shall add no less than fifty billion dollars to the gross national product of this country—and, most significant of all, this money will be added in the concentrated communities and in the rural South where the need is urgently greatest.

Another example of this new pragmatism I speak of, emerging from the church, is in the area of economics. In the Bible we read the story of Jesus feeding the five thousand with five loaves and a few fishes. I have believed if Jesus could feed five thousand with a few loaves and fishes and have twelve baskets full of food left over to feed the hungry, then the Christian church and those who are in the church could share our resources and feed the hungry, clothe the naked, and help provide opportunities for the poor.

A few years ago, two hundred members in the Zion Baptist Church in Philadelphia decided to put the Scriptures to a test and pool our resources to provide assistance and uplift to the underprivileged and the needy, as well as to create a way to leave benefits for generations coming after us. We wanted to do this within the framework of free enterprise, and at the same time "give" as well as "receive." So, these two hundred members, for thirty-six months, began to invest ten dollars a month in what we called the "10-36 Plan." The collections began. The result was phenomenal. Within a single year sufficient money had been collected to build a million-dollar garden apartment complex, using Black technicians, plumbers, electrical workers, and masons for the first time on a building project of that magnitude, built by Blacks in Philadelphia's history.

The second year, sufficient money had been put into the fund that one day a Black couple went to rent an apartment in an all-White apartment house and were refused. They came back and told us. The next week we bought the apartment house. After three years, the group had grown to six hundred investors, and we were able to build, with conventional mortgages, a two million-dollar shopping center, the first and largest shopping center built by Blacks in the nation. The center, called "Progress Plaza," stands on the main street of Philadelphia as tangible evidence of how people, sharing their resources together, can develop enterprises of economic significance.

The 10-36 Plan has now enrolled six thousand members in the Philadelphia area, with four thousand people on a waiting list, and has been responsible for initiating factories, developing a chain of inner-city food markets, and buying office buildings and other properties; it will return dividends to the children and children's children of investors for years and years to come.

This is a part of the new pragmatism evolving out of the Black church today. It is not Black capitalism, for there is no such thing · as Black capitalism—*capital is green!* But this new revolution of self-help is the work of a new awareness in the church of God that will, *in time,* become the main thrust in the Black and minority American communities across the nation. In time, "10-36," taken from the Bible and rooted in faith and prayer (and the willingness of participants to give, as well as to receive), will, I foresee, grow one day into one of the most important mutual cooperative programs of this century. In time hundreds of thousands of people, Black and White, will become a part of this kind of great new effort, leading to the rebuilding of entire communities, helping in the desegregation of all-White suburbs. They will create newfound resources to give many, many underprivileged and poor, who feel outside of the system, a glimmer of hope and new expectations for tomorrow. This kind of thrust will cause big business to realize the importance of human dividends. And this is important, because American business must change its views regarding its role in society. American industry cannot do business as usual. Changes have to be made. The times and the needs of the times dictate that changes have to be made. American business, in order to survive, will have to make human dividends equal in importance to capital dividends.

I accepted membership in the Board of General Motors Company, hoping that by my presence, I could speak to the need for human dividends in industrial enterprises. Happily, it seems that my fellow constituents on the General Motors Board are listening. *I shall keep on talking.* I am talking about matters like better opportunities for Blacks, Chicanos, Puerto Ricans, and even poor Whites in America; I am talking about human freedom for Blacks in the Union of South Africa, and for other oppressed people in the world. I think some progress is being made. We shall see what we shall see. I shall keep talking.

What I am saying is that, in spite of the shame of America, and in spite of the inequities of America, we are not giving up. Something is going to happen, because we are going to see that something happens. The forces of God are on the move. It is the new pragmatism. It is the new message of the Christian church saying: "So faith by itself, if it has no works, is dead" (James 2:17). And this new pragmatism, this new self-help spirit, being seen in the Black Christian community, as in the case of OIC, and as in the case of "10-36" *and other efforts,* will one day mean the survival of the nation.

In the midst of the violence and the racism and the shame of America—in spite of it all, because God lives, *I see hope.* And I know that if we will work and pray and trust in God, there will be freedom ahead.

I say to you here, and to all America today: "Do not despair! God is not dead! Take new courage. Take our hands, and help in this new self-help revolution that will spread like a wave across the nation." I ask you: "Take our hands!" But if you do not take our hands, we shall not stop; we shall keep on going! We shall keep on going until the benefits of America, and of the world, are fully ours. For we believe that God is with us.

We are determined to reach our goal. And in doing so, we shall save our children, and in so doing we shall save America. And we shall change the cries in our streets from "Burn, Baby, Burn" to "BUILD, BROTHER, BUILD." Take my hand and walk with us to this NEW DAY!

Alternatives to Despair

Speech given at dinner meeting of Columbia Broadcasting System (CBS), Doral Hotel, Miami, Florida, January 28, 1972

The greatness of our nation has been her ability to solve her most pressing problems. In the past, when faced with grave situations, the nation has consistently responded with workable solutions. She has done so in all aspects of our development, from spreading her frontiers to building great cities, to developing her technology, to putting a man on the moon and bringing him back to earth again. Since the days of our founding fathers, America's greatness has been in her ability to solve problems.

Tonight I want to present you with the greatest problem facing America today; and it is not the election of a president, the state of the economy, the war in Vietnam, or even pollution. Rather, the greatest problem facing America today is: "What to do with the Black man?" What is the nation going to do with her citizens of color, and how can they become equal participants in the democratic mainstream of the American way of life?

This is the Number One problem of the nation. If we can solve this problem, if we can make America truly America for everyone, Black, as well as White, then the American flag will fly with new meaning around the world, and challenges to our American way of life will lose most of their power. The rest of the world (the majority of which is nonwhite) is not strongly against democracy or against the free enterprise system, but rather against the way America treats her Black citizens. The world is saying to America, "There is nothing wrong with democracy, but why don't you practice at home what you preach?"

The test of democracy, in the eyes of the world, lies in the treatment of our colored minorities. In the future the rise and the fall of the nation could well depend upon this.

On the home front the importance of solving the problem of "what to do with the Black man" looms even greater than on the world front, because our failure to respond with workable solutions to this matter will have devastating effects on the future of us all here at home—economically, socially, and politically.

Economically there are dire implications. There are thirty million Black citizens in America today. By the year 2000, just thirty years from now, this number will increase to fifty million. By that time, one-half of all the jobs being done by my people will not even exist, for new kinds of technical jobs will have taken their place.

If there is no effort of extraordinary proportions begun to deal with the situation through massive training programs and unrestricted job opportunities, one out of every two Black Americans, by the year 2000, will have to be subsidized through public or social welfare.

At today's costs, it requires $3,000 to sustain and provide for one person on relief for one year. Simple mathematics tells us that by the year 2000 the cost of welfare for Blacks alone, at today's cost, will exceed $75 billion. Add to that number fifty million nonblacks who will not be prepared or able to secure or hold jobs, and we realize the total welfare bill, thirty years from today, could exceed $200 billion. This represents one-half of the total federal budget for the entire operation of the United States government at this time.

But, beyond that, there is a matter that disturbs me as a Black man even more than the cost of welfare payments. I am disturbed that twenty-five million of my Black brothers and sisters would become wards of the state, with the government telling us what to wear, what to eat, how many children to have, and where to live. Such dictatorial control as this raises the question of survival. Any government that can so control the lives of its dependent people can through that very control take away the lives of those same people.

A number of years ago, at the invitation of the West German government, I traveled through the redeveloping Germany to see what was going on there. Of all the experiences on that trip, one stands out in my mind—my visit to a concentration camp. I saw there at firsthand what can happen when the government gains control over the affairs and the lives of men. I cannot risk the possibility of anything like this ever happening to *my* people. Black men and women must become self-dependent, productive, and free of welfare for their survival. We must not have to depend upon the state for our existence; a man can never be free in a

113

democracy when his name is on the welfare rolls. Therefore, from a selfish point of view, the matter of the inclusion of the Black man in the democratic mainstream of the American way of life, and upgrading him economically, becomes imperative to me.

Also, the problem of the inclusion of the Black man must be solved for the survival of our cities. If we are not successful in dealing with the urban situation, by the end of the century nearly every large city in this country will become a gigantic Black ghetto, falling apart in decay, chaos, delinquency, and crime. It will not do to explain away this gloomy prospect by saying that Blacks are genetically criminal or violent, because they are not. They are no more so than anyone else would be in the same repressive situations. People are people. Conditions make men act as they do, rather than the men themselves.

Great invisible walls surround my people in our cities—invisible walls of segregation and prejudice and humiliation. As our numbers grow, by birth and migration, the invisible walls move out bit by bit, but they still surround us, holding us in, compressing us more and more in the most deplorable of conditions. Compression creates agitation, and agitation creates combustion, and combustion leads to violence.

If discrimination and segregation in housing do not come to an end within this generation, I predict that by the year 2000 our big cities will turn into centers of military occupation, and the U.S. Army (in the name of peace, law and order, and national security) will be stationed in every city. I predict that urban guerilla warfare, sporadic at first, will break out across the nation and will grow in intensity until the country is driven to the brink of racial revolution.

Also, the problem must be solved for political and ideological reasons; otherwise I can foresee the day when the American people will voluntarily give up democracy for a totalitarian government to deal with an increasingly chaotic situation.

We have already seen evidence of what terrible things can happen on a small scale in some of our cities, even as they are now. These are but a small indication of what can happen in the future on an even wider scale. Millions and millions of young Black children are now growing up who will not be satisfied with anything less than full opportunity and full equal rights. No half-way measures will do for them, and there will be millions and millions of young White children standing by their sides.

Considering all, we must begin now, more intently and massively than ever, to move constructively toward the solution of this American problem as it affects the Black man before destruction and terror engulfs us all. The heartening part is that something can be done about the situation. The problem is not insolvable. *There are alternatives to despair.* To be sure, the alternatives and the solutions are not short-term things. The Black man and the White man will not be brought together in unity in America for some time to come. The division between us is too deep for simple and quick answers. But at some point we must begin to bridge the gap perceptibly, believing that in time we can Americanize America and save it for everyone.

My alternatives to despair call for bold efforts on the part of those who want to see the changes come.

We must all realize that the problem of racial division and discrimination in America cannot and will not be solved by the White man alone, nor by the Black man alone, but by the efforts of the Black and White man together. As a cart cannot roll on one wheel, because it needs two, so the solution to the problem of the Black man in America is not the White man's problem alone, nor the Black man's problem alone, but it is the problem of both; and to the extent that each plays his part will we arrive at the ultimate solution.

I, therefore, tonight, ask for a new American deal of the White man and the Black man in this country. I do not ask White Americans to forget their prejudices, because I know that only God can make a man do that, but I ask White Americans to cease denying to Black Americans the full rights of the Constitution as provided for all Americans. I do not ask White Americans to love me, because I know that only God can make a man do that, too, but I ask that White Americans not withhold from me my right as an American to move into a house where I want to move, and to live in a community where I want to live. I do not ask White Americans to welcome me into their homes. Let your home be your castle. But I ask them not to decide for me, on a basis of race, those with whom my children will socialize, where my children will go to school, and what neighborhood they will live in. I ask White America to take from around me these invisible walls of segregation that hem me into ghettos of decay, deprivation, and death.

I have no desire to be White. Being White is your problem! I just want to be a first-class American citizen with the same rights and privileges as every other American citizen to life, liberty, and the pursuit of happiness. I will not be satisfied with anything less than that—and I will continue to fight for it to the end, so help me God!

White America, I ask you to do your part! For one hundred years since the Emancipation Proclamation we have been segregated in job opportunities. Even now discrimination is rampant in American industry and in much of American government in the higher and more affluent jobs. I do not ask to be president of your companies or general manager of your plants. I know it will require time for that condition to come, but it is time for Black Americans to be upgraded from the broom-and-bucket brigades and the lowest paid jobs on the assembly lines into better job opportunities in factories and office buildings across the nation. The time is past for college graduates who are Black to have to be satisfied with being janitors, laborers, and the lowest paid employees in industry and government.

White America, I ask you to do your part. I appeal to industry to do the unusual, and in the name of corporate awareness to upgrade at least four Black to four Whites, for every job that opens up in the next year in blue-collar job classifications across the nation in every industry and business. I ask industry, if possible, to freeze for a year all salaried jobs that come about through attrition of White workers and to unfreeze Black workers so that they can fill those jobs. And where my people are not prepared, I ask you to train them to be prepared; because it is as easy to have on-the-job training for a supervisor with twenty years of experience in the plant as it is to have on-the-job training for a hard-core worker on the assembly line.

In particular I ask the broadcasting industry to follow through on what I am saying here, because the spotlight on minority employment will, in the next few years, be focused more brightly on you. Your industry is more in the public domain than most, and it uses the public airways for its services. There should be more Black faces in a room like this next year than now. Just one is not enough—it is not even token! CBS is going to have to get busy to do something about this problem and get busy now. This kind of bold effort by American industry will give my people assurance that American industry cares about us and that big business is as concerned about people as it is about profit. White America, I ask you to do your part!

I ask White America to treat me with humanity. My fellow Black man and I don't want to be regarded as "Boy" anymore— we want to be called and treated as men. Several years ago when Robert Kennedy came to see me in Philadelphia, as we rode from the airport, I jokingly said to him, "Gee, I'm glad to see you, boy." An instant frown covered his face, and he said to me with a reflex answer, "Don't call me boy!" For a second there was silence and then a smile, and we laughed about it and all was well. But at that moment Senator Kennedy instinctively said what Black people have been saying to themselves all their lives: "Don't call me boy!" No grown person wants to be treated like, or called, a boy. If he is twenty-one years of age, he is a man. If this is true for a president's brother, a senator of the United States government, and a millionaire, surely it is true for us! I ask you to do your part. Don't call me boy—nor treat me as a boy. Have respect for me and treat me as a man!

And if you do your part, I assure you this night that I will do my part. Speaking for those in this country who believe as I believe, we will do our part to see that the Black man in this country lifts himself by "self-help" to get out of the hole he is in, even if he did not dig it himself. If you will do your part, I pledge that in one hundred cities of America I will do my part.

OIC, the Opportunities Industrialization Center, by the year 1980, will train one million men and women in useful jobs and will take 300,000 people off relief rolls. OIC is the phenomenal self-help training program which began in Philadelphia eight years ago in an old jailhouse and which is giving hope to the hopeless and providing a way out for the tens of thousands of poor people every day all across the country. People who thought there was no hope are learning that "genius is color blind, and a man is like a balloon, for it is not his color that makes him rise, but what he has inside of him." If you will do your part, OIC will, by the year 2000, prepare ten million men and women for useful jobs through our training centers across the nation, and we will stem the tide of welfarism in America.

If you will do your part, we will do our part! In the next ten years, through OIC, we will train fifty thousand men and women to become entrepreneurs and managers of their own businesses, and through community investment cooperatives we will provide resources and technical help to assist these businesses to become successful. By the year 2000, we will make the Black man as much a productive part of the free enterprise system as any other ethnic or racial group in America.

I give to America tonight "Alternatives to Despair": to White America and Black America. The problem must be solved, and the problem can be solved if we work together. The time has come for us to put Black power and White power together, to build American power, in order that we might save the nation for everyone.

There are those who say to us there is no hope; things are too far gone. But I believe in America and I believe in you.

Particularly do I ask that you of the Columbia Broadcasting System, representing one of the most powerful media of influence in the nation and in the world, will use the strength of your industry to take this message of hope and of OIC to the nation. I ask you to utilize the materials that are now available about OIC from the National Advertising Council to let America know about OIC and what it can mean to all of us, and to urge America to support OIC so that it can do a real job for the country.

Let us join hands and move together. *Instead of emphasizing burning, now let us emphasize building!*

"Alternatives to Despair"—White America, you do your part, and we will do ours!

> A nation of opportunity
> Let us build, let us build!
> A nation of liberty
> Let us build, let us build!
> America for everyone—
> Let the message ring!
> A nation of brotherhood
> Let us build, let us build!

I See Freedom Ahead

Delivered on the occasion of the Lovejoy Award
August 23, 1971

Receiving this award is a great and distinguished honor. The Improved Benevolent Protective Order of Elks of the World is one of the greatest organizations of the Black race, and its leader, Hobson R. Reynolds, is one of the greatest leaders the race has ever produced. Thank you for this memorable honor.

Ask a Black man anywhere in the world what he wants most and his answer will be "freedom." Ask a Black man in Ghana what he wants most, and his answer will be "freedom." Ask a Black man in Kenya what he wants most, and his answer will be "freedom." In England, in the West Indies, in Harlem, in Chicago, or in New Orleans his answer will be the same. There is a global desire among Black men all around the world for freedom. We want to be free; and to us freedom means equal treatment as human beings everywhere in the world, without being held back because of the color of our skin.

Black men everywhere want the world to know that no longer will we be satisfied with things as they have been, and that we are determined to rise. We want the world to know that in the days ahead we will not be satisfied with anything less than full equal opportunity, full equal recognition, and full equal rights.

All over the world we want to be free. In Lagos, in Nairobi, in Johannesburg, in Harlem, in Watts, and on Beale Street, we want to be free. As Christians or as Muslims or as members of any other faith, we want to be free: free of discrimination, free of humiliation, free from the indignities of a world that has put a premium on being White and a penalty on being Black. Around the world we want to be free, and we are determined to be free, and we are *going* to be free!

The great matter before us now is not *"if,"* but *"how?"* How realistically can we get to the place where a Black child born anywhere in America can have the same opportunity to live a full and unrestricted life as a White child born at the same time in America?

Already great progress has been made in this direction. The immeasurable efforts of W. E. B. Du Bois, Thurgood Marshall, Roy Wilkins, Martin Luther King, Malcolm X, Whitney Young, and others have brought us to where we are today. But now, we must go on. We must go until real freedom for the Black man in America—and, one day, in the whole world—is truly a reality.

The freedom that we seek, of equal opportunity and unrestricted equal rights, will not come overnight in America or any other place in the world. But we know that it will come if we will work and plan for it. It will not come through emotionalism; it will not come through mass meetings; it will not come by marching or by making noise or by trying to burn the town down. All of these things might place attention on our problems, but they will not solve them. Realistically, the only way to solve our problems, at this point in our history, is by *planning* our future, clearly and objectively, and then working to make that plan a reality.

Nothing works for long without a plan. The race needs a plan.

We must not delude ourselves with false hopes. Equal opportunity and full recognition in a White-dominated world will not come easily. There will be no "freedom" now. The realities of our situation indicate that it will take years to right the wrongs we face today. So the race today needs a plan that will show us the direction to go and the means necessary to get there.

The plan must call for getting rid of some things that hold us back, and the first of these is superstition. There is too much superstition in the race. We cannot direct our youth to progress and discipline as long as, in such large numbers, we still believe in black magic, fortune-tellers, and "goofy dust." More and more we are finding that in this world even mysticism is a science. We have to get over our fright of the dark and the dead, and realize that it is not the dead we should worry about, but the living. Dead men can't hurt you, but the living can.

The plan must call for getting rid of our fear. In spite of all Dr. Martin Luther King did to give us courage, millions of our people are still afraid to speak up for their rights and to test the hundreds of new laws that have been written as a result of great sacrifices, providing the Black man with protection against discrimination and segregation. For this reason, discrimination and segregation continue to abound in the land. Say what you will, the main reason that segregation continues to exist in housing and employment and educational opportunities in America today is fear: the fear of Black people to speak up and to stand up for their rights. As long as you are afraid to move out and to test anti-discrimination laws that prohibit segregation in housing, so long will all-White suburbs remain segregated; as long as you are afraid to ask for upgrading of job opportunities on the jobs where you work, so long will you remain where you are; as long as you fail in our hometowns to test the Supreme Court ruling that public schools in America, South and North, must desegregate, so long will the majority of the public schools continue to comply with only token integration, and most schools in Black communities will remain all Black, unequal, and inferior.

Above all, the Afro must get rid of his fears and stand up for his rights. Today, at last, the law is on our side. Therefore we must use the law and test the law. We must keep the Commissions on Human Relations and the courts working overtime across America. If we will do this, and if we will speak up and stand up for our rights as Americans, walls of discrimination will come tumbling down. As before men used the law to keep us back, now we must use the law to move us forward.

The plan must call for getting rid of our feelings of inferiority. Nobody is going to believe in you if you don't believe in yourself! For three hundred years we Black people have been told we were inferior, so much so that we believe it ourselves. The vast majority of us believe that we are inferior to White people and that "White is right, Brown—stick around, and Black—get back." It is what we have been taught to believe in the books we have read, in the movies we have seen, and in the shows on television. We have even been taught in the food that we eat, because white cake is called "angel food," and black cake is called "devil's food"! We have been brainwashed; we need a new kind of heritage education to unbrainwash ourselves. We must rid the race of inferiority feelings, because nothing can hold us back more than lack of confidence. We must believe in ourselves as Black people.

We must teach our children to be like one of those two Black boys who were watching a jet plane fly overhead. One little boy said, "Oh, I wish I was White so I could fly that plane like that White boy!" But the other Black boy replied, "If that White boy will give me the throttle, I will fly it, as Black as I am!"

We must build self-confidence in our youth and in our race. To the extent that we build confidence, we can move mountains.

The plan must call for racial unity. Black people fight each other too much; we can't seem to get together. Let us stop fighting each other and build a leadership of integrity that we all can follow. We *must* work together, realizing that there is always more strength in things that are together than in things that are apart. Even in poker two pairs will always beat two kings, and a straight flush, all like cards together, will always beat four aces.

The race needs *unity* in purchasing power. The annual purchasing power of the Black man in America today exceeds $30 billion. We must harness that purchasing power and use it in such a way that no business, large or small, would dare close its doors to the equal employment of our people. If we could harness our purchasing power, anyone who tried to impose job discrimination on us would be inviting a national boycott of his products.

The availability of power can be tantamount to the use of it. We may never have to use it, but it is good to know that we have it. No company, however large, can withstand a selective patronage boycott by the Black man in America, properly organized and sustained.

The plan must call for the strongest possible emphasis on education. The entire race must point itself toward preparation. The key to opportunity in the future will be education. This means we must put more emphasis on training our brains than on kicking our heels.

The Black man was born at the equator, which is the balancing point of the earth. By nature he possesses a balanced mind. It is up to us Blacks to decide what we do with our minds. Either we can do nothing with them and become a race of "dependables" and "know nothings," or we can use our minds and stretch them and train them and master the technical, artistic, and social knowledge of the world.

Ignorance is our greatest enemy. Freedom requires self-discipline, and ignorance is not capable of self-discipline.

If we do not develop our minds and skills, starting from the cradle, the Black man, by the year 2000, will be a ward of the state. One-third of the race will be on relief, and the government will have virtual control of our lives. Our large cities will be concentration camps for Black people, Puerto Ricans, and Mexican Americans; and a despot in the name of "national security" and "law and order" will be able to emerge on the scene and start a movement for the elimination of the "problem," which would mean the elimination of the Black man in America. This may sound like folly to you, but it happened just a few years ago to the Jew in Germany, and it could be attempted against the Black man in America.

This is why a program like OIC, the Opportunities Industrialization Center, has to succeed. OIC has a goal to train one hundred thousand men and women in new skills each year for the next ten years until we have trained one million Blacks, Chicanos, and Puerto Ricans, and placed them in good well-paying jobs. OIC has to succeed for the future security of our race. We cannot afford to depend on the government for our survival.

As a matter of fact, we must go further than training for jobs. In the next ten years OIC must reach every Black home with a message of *self-help* and *progress*. We must stress learning in every home, cleanliness in every home, the value of time in every home, self-pride in every home, respect for Black women in every home, and the importance of Black women respecting *themselves* in every home. We must stress honesty in every home, morality in every home, and the maintenance of the health of our bodies in every home. We must teach that the wrong use of drugs is an abomination to the race. And above all, we must strive for the solidarity of every Black home.

We must plan ahead in politics. The Black people of America are potentially the most powerful voting bloc in the nation, but we have less political strength in the nation, states, and cities than virtually any other major ethnic group: less than the Irish, the Italian, the Jew—you name it! Very few major political decisions include the Black American; for all these years he has had to be satisfied with "crumbs from the table."

One reason why communities where Blacks live in large numbers are so run down is that we have so little muscle at City Hall. Except for some token representation, as far as the major

124

political parties are concerned in our big cities, we just aren't there. The only time people downtown seem to pay any attention to us is when we decide to "raise hades" or when election time comes.

All of this must be changed. The Black man must become able to exert political strength equal to his political potential. In order for "the man" to know that we really mean business, we have to learn to "rack him up" at the polls.

We must, therefore, plan and work for a new political awakening also. We must make voter registration a major priority of the Black race. We must not only register—we must vote, even if we have to be carried to the polls on stretchers. But not only must we vote; we must, also, learn *how* we vote. The day has come for the Black man to practice political independence. The day of being all-Republican or all-Democrat has come to an end. Neither party is going to do any more for you and me than they have to do. The race would not be in the mess it is in today if the major political parties had operated with a broader motivation than mere self-interest. In the future we must see to it that the Black man's vote is not in anybody's pocket. We must vote Democrat when it is in our interest to vote Democrat, and Republican when it is in our interest to vote Republican. And we must be willing to form our own parties when it is necessary to do that, too. We have long heard it said that the Democrats are for the "poor people" and the Republicans are for the "rich people." Don't fool yourselves. Both of them have been for the same thing: "Winning elections!"

We have been politically blind, and everybody has been taking advantage of us. It is time across America that we opened our eyes. We must zig when we have to zig, and zag when we have to zag! We must let both Democrats and Republicans know that in the future we will support those who support us and turn on those who turn on us. Let the White man know his political games with Black people are over; let him know our eyes are opening. Whereas "before we were blind, now we see!"

In the 1972 election both parties will need the Black vote to win. The Democrats will need it, or they won't have a ghost of a chance to win. The Republicans will need at least two million Black votes to be returned to the White House because the Democrats will be united as never before, and the majority of the 18-year-old votes will go Democratic. So if ever there was a time for Mr. Nixon to "produce," it is now. Already some moves have been made in this direction, not enough—but some. More Blacks have been appointed to high office in this government than ever before, and some other requests are being heeded, at last. To be sure, the government has not given OIC the $100 million a year it needs to do its work in one hundred cities. Nevertheless, it has to be acknowledged that this government *has* given OIC $32 million to do its work for this year in America, and a million dollars through the Agency for International Development for OIC work in Africa in the countries of Nigeria, Ghana, Ethiopia, and Kenya. Anytime any administration gives a Black man $30 million to carry on his work, it deserves credit, particularly when the Black man getting the money is a Black Baptist preacher. I am hoping now that we will be able to get the $68 million more that we need, but $32 million is progress.

But the federal government must do much more, because the problem is so vast. There are twenty-five million Blacks in America and one-third of us still live beneath the poverty line. There are also millions of Chicanos and Puerto Ricans and American Indians, who are no better off than the Black American, and sometimes worse off. So we want the president to turn to the Black man in America, and to the Brown man and the Yellow man and the Red man, to help us significantly in our need. We applaud Mr. Nixon's trips abroad. But we want him to take a trip to Louisiana or Alabama and help get Black people accepted into the United States of America. We want to see Mr. Nixon get wrapped up in Black people in America as much as he is getting wrapped up in Chinese people in China and Russian people in Russia.

I repeat, this is the beginning of a new day in Black politics. Those who help us, we shall help them. Things will not be as they have been before. We shall vote on the basis of results, and not just promises. In the future we shall challenge the politicians: "Show us what you have done!" Whereas, before we were blind, now we see.

Finally, we must plan ahead for economic productivity. We will have to learn to pool our resources for the mutual development of the race, and thereby also help the nation. We must create a cooperative plan in which every Black man and woman, every boy and girl can participate in every city, town, and hamlet in America. We must create a cooperative plan whereby out of our own personal resources, however small, a "treasury of the people" can be established to provide our own capital funds to back up our own Black-owned and developed enterprises all across the nation. Instead of just talking about how we Black people should get something of our own, we must create a plan to put our money where our mouth is.

A formula called the "10-36 Plan" already has been successfully tested in Philadelphia. In this plan six thousand people put ten dollars a month into a "treasury of the people" for thirty-six months to build enterprises owned by our own people. As a result of this plan in Philadelphia, we own a shopping center, food chain stores, apartment houses, office buildings, and factories. The same thing can be done all over America, if we really want to do it! The Black man must own something of his own. *In the future we will have to learn how to help hold the world up, and not lean upon it!*

The cry of the sixties was "Burn, Baby, Burn!" Let us make the cry of the seventies "Build, Brother, Build!"

Black America, I can see freedom ahead, planning, working, learning, praying; I can see freedom ahead.

Black America, I can see freedom ahead, striving, saving, building, lifting; I can see freedom ahead.

Black America, I can see freedom ahead. With faith and hope and pride and unity, we shall walk into a new day.

Black America, I can see freedom ahead!

4
OIC
INTERNATIONAL

When I wrote *Build Brother Build,* I expressed a dream, but I was not sure when it would be fulfilled, probably not in the next generation nor in my lifetime:

> When I plan for the future, my thoughts turn eventually to Africa. Somehow, I believe, slavery will be turned to the advantage of our future. The day will come when the continent from which my forefathers came will blossom into a paradise. I have a feeling that my ultimate freedom and my ultimate security are tied to the development of Africa. Of course I have no intention of forsaking America, for America is my home and I have helped to build her and shape her. But like the Jew and others who came to make this country what it is, I need an anchor in the past, a place my children can proudly call their ancestral home. My citizenship is here, but a part of my spirit is in Africa, also.
>
> I envision a bridge from America to Africa over which one day my children and my Black brothers and Black sisters will move freely from one side to the other and back again. The Bible has said, "The day will come when Ethiopia shall stretch forth her hands again," and I know that day is coming, though I shall not live to see it. The time is not far off when Black technicians, artisans and craftsmen by the thousands and tens of thousands will visit a flourishing Africa, helping to mold that continent into a greatness glorious to see.[1]

[1] Leon H. Sullivan, *Build Brother Build* (Philadelphia: Macrae Smith Company, 1969), pp. 178-179.

Now I am sure that all this will happen; in fact, it has already begun. While I may not witness the fulfillment of this most inevitable reality in my lifetime, the process has already begun. It will take time, but it shall come to pass, for "nothing is more powerful than an idea whose time has come."

The fate and destiny of the Afro-American is entwined inseparably with the African continent and its people. We are intimately interwoven not just by Black consciousness based on historical experiences, but by Black survival and the necessity of Black solidarity, development, and growth. Only the Black people the world over, working together, can achieve real life in the warmth of the sun and in the presence of God.

In 1969, I made my first "return" journey to Africa. By choice I landed first on the soil of Ethiopia. The Bible had told me the time would come when Ethiopia shall stretch forth her hand unto God (see Psalm 68:31). Therefore, I wanted my pilgrimage to the continent of Africa to start there. As I descended the steps of the plane, I knew God was in this visit with me. As I placed my feet on African soil and knelt to the earth to kiss the ground, I said to myself, "Back after three hundred years!" I was back—and I knew even then that hundreds and thousands and perhaps millions like me would follow. It is in God's divine providence that we shall return by the millions to visit, to labor, to help build, as well as learn from this great continent. As the Jews see their Israel, the Irish their Ireland, the Italians their Italy, so will the Black man see his Africa. We will not necessarily transfer our citizenship, but we will share our resources, our ambitions, our hopes, and our common destiny. I am aware that this is a unique and arduous purpose for a returned son to fulfill.

When the first OIC was begun in that old abandoned jailhouse in Philadelphia in 1964, my concern was initially America—Black America. There was and is so much to be done in America, so much still needed. Although I thought of the implications even then of the work for Africa, Latin

America, and Asia, still I made no effort to pursue it, for the needs at home were themselves too great.

By 1967 my timetable for involvement in Africa started changing rapidly. This sudden involvement was the result of one man I have since come to know, love, and respect, Dr. Folorunso Salawu, a Nigerian physician. Dr. Salawu, who was concerned with his Lagos community's growing unemployment problem and its negative social ramification, learned of OIC through reading a 1965 issue of *Reader's Digest* and wrote to me expressing an interest in the OIC work. Dr. Salawu felt that maybe OIC would be the vehicle to assist him and other concerned citizens in tackling the increasing unemployment problem of Lagos.

As the result of Dr. Salawu's letter, as well as others from Ghana, Kenya, Ethiopia, and other African countries requesting that OICs be established, OIC is now in the process,

132

with strong support from the United States Agency for International Development (USAID), of assisting private citizens' groups develop OIC programs in Nigeria, Ghana, Ethiopia, and Kenya.

With strong local leadership expressing a realistic concern for the private citizen to play a more involved role in the responsibility for national development, the OIC concept and methods were transferred to the African soil. Leaders such as Dr. Salawu, of Nigeria, Geormbeeyi Adali-Mortty, John Moses, and S. P. Dampson, of Ghana, Drs. Selashe Kebede and Abebe Ambatchew, of Ethiopia, and Messrs. A. O. Menya, Godfrey Tetu, and Chris Malavu, of Kenya, are the reasons OIC, an Afro-American program, has returned to the continent of its "origin." These are some of our brothers concerned about our people who pulled me irreversibly back to Africa, the land of my heritage.

Not only did I receive inquiries from Africa, but letters of interest came from Latin America and Asia as well. Now we are in the process of trying to help struggling communities in Belize (British Honduras) and in the Dominican Republic to establish OIC programs under the leadership of the Reverend Martin C. Avila and Dr. Elias Santana, respectively. We have the manpower and the know-how; what we are lacking in assuring proper assistance to this growing international interest in OIC is finances—but with God's continuous assistance and guidance, we will find a way, we will make a way. We developing people have no other choice.

To assist my African brothers properly, I need two important things: first, an organizational structure capable of planning, developing, and implementing relevant OIC programs modified to the varied conditions of local international communities; and second, realistic and practical leadership for such OIC components as are charged with internationalizing the movement.

In the OIC program I had noticed a quiet and intent young man with what I perceived to be a sensitive and meditative interest in the future of Africa and people of African origin throughout the world. I have seen so many neo-black, pro-Afro phonies seeking an escapism through an illusion of so-called African identity, that to see a youth with his head set squarely on his shoulders about the subject was a significant and welcome sight. I determined that this young man would be my Paul in the African mission.

This young man whom I chose to lead the newly established African OIC component known as OIC International was named Valo JorDan, later to be changed, as he said, to his correct name, Valfoulaye Diallo. Young Diallo had youth, training, experience, and endurance. He was a long distance runner in college; he had studied international and African affairs; and he had lived, worked, and traveled not only extensively in Africa but in Latin America, Asia, and Europe as well. I knew he had the stamina, training, and experience

134

for this assignment and great dedication for the future of Africa. Therefore, I invited him to work with me in the development of this work.

Since my initial trip to the African continent during February and March, 1969, I have returned there on two other occasions. In addition to Ethiopia, I have visited Kenya, Nigeria, and Ghana, also making brief stops in Uganda, Liberia, and Senegal. During these return visits to Mother Africa, I had the opportunity to visit such great institutions as the Organization of African Unity (OAU), the Economic Commission for Africa (ECA), and the Nigerian Institute of International Affairs. I have met great African leaders and statesmen, such as Diallo Telli, Secretary General of OAU; Dr. Robert Gardiner, Executive Secretary of ECA; Emperor Haile Selassie of Ethiopia; the Honorable Mbiyu Koinange; Mwai Kibaki; the late Tom Mboya; Major General Yakubu Gowan; and many others. Visiting these places and meeting these people deepened my understanding of the African reality and my necessary commitment to the continent. It also afforded me the opportunity to explain and discuss with them the OIC program. These men all blessed and endorsed the program and encouraged its development in Africa.

Upon meeting the leadership of Africa, one of the first things one notices in this new dynamic leadership that is leading and developing Africa is its youth. Many of the leaders controlling and guiding the destiny in many of the developing countries in Africa were my age and younger. If they were not young in age, they were certainly youthful in their thoughts and desires for a new Africa and a better life for their people.

His Excellency Emperor Haile Selassie, one of the greatest African statesmen, has not only played a major role in the survival process of the African continent but also is one of the chief architects of the new development that is underway in Africa. He along with Kwame Nkrumah and many other dynamic African leaders brought into creation the Organiza-

tion of African Unity. He has also assisted in eliminating and lessening internal continental conflict and disagreements among African countries. When I had the opportunity to meet the Emperor, I was accompanied by Dr. Salawu, the Chairman of the OIC Nigerian Project, as well as Valfoulaye Diallo, my international director. During this meeting I had the pleasure of discussing and explaining to him in detail the OIC program and its purpose and how we were interested in working with a local Ethiopian group in developing a similar program in Ethiopia. The Emperor greeted us most warmly and indicated his full endorsement and support for the development of OIC in Ethiopia.

During my 1971 visit to Africa, I also had the honor to join with my brother Diallo Telli once again. On this and previous occasions, he has continuously expressed his interest and admiration not only for the OIC program, but also for what the Black Americans are doing in America and throughout the world, particularly for their growing interest and expression of Africa. For example, he told me:

> I would like to seize the opportunity of your stay with us in Addis Ababa to reiterate to you our deep appreciation for the active role that you have played since 1964 thru the Opportunities Industrialization Center in helping Africans get the necessary training to enable them to earn their living and dignity, and to assume full responsibility in the process of development of their respective countries. Furthermore, the establishment and success of OIC can contribute to shattering the myth long disseminated by colonial powers that Africans are subhuman, that they are totally incapable of reaching the same standards of Europeans. The success of OIC, if there is need of proof, shows that Black men can achieve anything that other races can achieve.

You can imagine how thrilled and delighted I was in receiving these encouraging and reassuring words from such a great man as Diallo Telli. They serve as a continuous source of inspiration for me and my people to struggle even harder. He went on to say that if OIC is to make even a greater contribution to Africa, it should consider expanding the program throughout the whole continent. He indicated that it would be most advisable for OIC to diversify its sphere of action to all

of the continent irrespective of language areas and political options. I am in full agreement with this. It is my earnest desire to fulfill this advice as received from Diallo Telli and to see, with the agreement of the African people and countries, that OIC is established in every country throughout the continent to play its role and responsibility in assisting our brothers and sisters in creating a better life.

In an earlier visit I also had the privilege of meeting another important and dynamic figure in the African movement. That person was Dr. Robert Gardiner, a Ghanaian, Executive Secretary of ECA. Dr. Gardiner, like many of the other African leaders I had met, expressed a keen interest in the possibilities of OIC in Africa and the role that it could play. Dr. Gardiner said to me during my visit, "Your coming here has been a godsend, and our talks have given me considerable courage. The principles and programs of the Opportunities Industrialization Center are very similar to the projects that ECA is promoting in Africa." He continued by saying, "I am sure the cooperation between the Commission and OIC will be to our mutual advantage."

Dr. Gardiner went on to propose that he would like to send one of the senior members of ECA to Philadelphia to study the OIC program and this was accomplished. From July, 1969, to July, 1970, Dr. Kidane M. Zerezghi, Director of Small-Scale Industry for ECA, was assigned to Philadelphia by Dr. Gardiner for orientation and training in operation and works of OIC. Ever since our meeting, Dr. Gardiner has continued to give his encouragement and blessings to OIC programs developing in the various African countries and has also given assistance and advice to our efforts personally and through his staff.

Also, I would like to mention the brotherly meeting that I had with the late Tom Mboya. I think that Africa will never recover from the loss of such a great son. He was such a dynamic individual, full of energy and dedication to the African cause. His loss is felt not only in Africa but also in the

139

whole Black world. Nevertheless his spirit and dedication continue to inspire us.

I had the opportunity of meeting young Tom on several occasions to explain and discuss with him the OIC program and the interest we had received from local Kenya citizens wishing to establish such a program in his country. At this time Tom was serving as Minister for the Ministry of Economic Planning and Development in Kenya. He expressed his interest in the OIC program, indicating that he would welcome the concept of a training center based on the ideas I had explained to him. He went on to assure me that he was very much pleased with the interest and effort that Afro-Americans have been making to get interested and involved in the development of the new African countries.

I have also had the opportunity of getting to know Tom's family, including his lovely wife, Pamela, and his two brothers, Alphonso Okuku, who is working with ECA, and young Peter, who had worked in our OIC program in America.

While in Kenya I also had the pleasure of meeting the Honorable Mbiyu Koinange of the Office of the President. He serves as the Minister of State and is a close companion to President Kenyatta. He expressed a very keen interest in OIC and its development in Kenya. He, like many of the other African leaders, was very keen on Black Americans playing a more dynamic role in assisting Africa toward its fulfillment. He indicated that if Black Americans are seriously committed to helping their motherland, "they must come now and they must come quickly." He let it be known that Kenya would be definitely interested in having her African sisters and brothers from America contribute to Kenya's development.

Traveling from East Africa to West, I had the pleasure and the honor of meeting the Head of State of Nigeria, General Yakubu Gowan, a young leader who has a great deal to offer not only to the development of Nigeria, but also to all of Africa. At that time a terrible civil conflict was raging in

140

Nigeria, and I was greatly moved by his depth of sensitivity and sincerity toward retaining Nigeria as one united country and ending the war as expeditiously as possible. Because he was such a busy man, I was surprised but pleased that our scheduled twenty-five-minute audience developed into over an hour's discussion. Not only did we discuss the OIC program and its possible development in Nigeria, which he warmly endorsed, but we also had time to discuss the problems of Nigeria's unity. We discussed how the war could have negative ramifications throughout the entire continent if the unity of Nigeria was not preserved. I also took a message back to President Nixon from General Gowan to make him better understand the situation in Nigeria and the position of its leaders.

I indicated then, and I said it on many occasions before and after, that I was deeply concerned about Nigeria and committed to the principle of "one Nigeria." I think that history has taught us that to allow further balkanization of the continent would not be to the advantage of our brothers and sisters in Nigeria and elsewhere in Africa, nor the African people throughout the world. Now that the war is over, I am pleased it has come to an end with Nigeria intact, moving toward rapid reunification. A unified Nigeria is important because I see Nigeria more and more playing a dynamic leadership role in the major effort of moving the continent more rapidly toward continental unity.

Let me indicate here that there are many voices talking about and disagreeing with the concept and possibilities of continental unity in Africa. With all my soul and being, I believe and know a unified Africa is possible and will be realized. The only thing it would take to achieve this objective is for all of us of African descent to believe 100 percent in its inevitability, no matter what distant and foreign voices are saying. If we have belief and confidence in this possibility, it can and will be achieved. Just as with OIC, one of the major problems of Black people is that of attitude. I think

143

this problem looms even larger for all African people. Once we arrive at the attitude that African unity is possible and definitely necessary for our being, it will be achieved. I know that there are many others like myself, both in Africa and throughout the African world, who share this common destiny, and this attitude will enlarge itself until it has engulfed all African people.

From Nigeria I traveled to Ghana, where I had the opportunity to meet with the then Head of State, General Ankrah, in the Osu Castle, his official residence. The castle is a vivid reminder of those influences that are responsible for the presence of African people, including myself, throughout the Western world. Captive Africans were held and shipped from this castle into slavery.

Not only did General Ankrah take a keen interest in learning about OIC, but also he extended to me and to the local OIC Ghana committee that was developing the local program his own personal endorsement and that of the Ghana government. That support has continued under the present regime in Ghana.

July 4, 1970, was another historic step in the internationalization of the OIC movement. It was historic not only in the sense that July 4 is the day American independence is celebrated, but also on this day in 1970 I departed for Africa accompanied by forty OIC people representing many and various OICs throughout America. We were going back "home" to Africa as a group not only to tour this great continent, but also in another small but unique way to make a contribution toward the land of our ancestry. The main purpose of this trip was threefold:

1. A larger group of Afro-Americans would have a direct experience and contact with Africa, particularly those Americans that worked in the OIC programs.
2. By leading this delegation to Africa, we felt that in addition to just having contact with Africa, these Afro-Americans could participate in contributing toward a better un-

derstanding between America and Africa, especially relationships between Africans and Afro-Americans.

3. This group, for the short time they were in Africa, would share their experience of OIC with the local people who were attempting to implement similar programs in two West African countries.

We went first to Nigeria, where we had the opportunity of meeting with our local counterparts as well as government officials and private industrialists, and experienced the daily lives of our brothers and sisters in the country. We attended lectures and discussions at the University of Lagos, and we were able to visit, dine, and discuss a whole host of things with the everyday Nigerian citizen. We also had the chance to travel to various parts of Nigeria outside the capital, such as Ibadan, Abeokuta, and Ikare.

From Nigeria we proceeded on to Ghana, where we received a similar brotherly greeting. We were met at the airport by a large delegation of local OIC members. My wife, Grace, was presented with a bouquet of roses by a pretty little Ghanaian girl. The warmth that we had encountered in Nigeria was truly continuing in Ghana. We had the opportunity to meet again with not only local OIC counterparts but also government officials and private industrialists. We visited the University of Ghana where we attended lectures and discussions on the history and development of Ghana in particular and Africa in general. We also traveled outside the capital city of Accra to such places as Tema, Cape Coast, and Elmina. I think that one of the greatest experiences that any Black American could have would be to visit the castle in Elmina where many of our people were held until they were transported out of the African continent into slavery in the Western world. The stories told by the guards of the castle were so moving that they brought some members of our delegation to tears. But, above and beyond this, the visit to Elmina provided us with another vivid understanding of our historical connection to the African continent.

It would be impossible for me to close this brief section on Africa without paying tribute to those sons of Africa who work and labor in the U.S. representing their countries. It has been my pleasure and privilege to get to know such great men as Ambassador Ebenezer M. Debrah, of Ghana, who has been a great inspiration to the OIC movement in the United States and to many other similar Black organizations in America. He has actively demonstrated and voiced his concern, commitment, and support for solving the problems of Black Americans. I don't think there is any other ambassador who has actively demonstrated such a brotherly spirit to the African population that resides in America. I have also had the pleasure of knowing Ambassador Leonard Kibinge, of Kenya, as well as Ambassador Joe Iyalla, of Nigeria. Both of these men have been quite encouraging to the OIC development in their respective countries and continue to give strong support and endorsement for the development of OIC programs. And I have also had the opportunity to meet with Ambassador Dr. Minasse Haile, who represents the oldest independent African country, Ethiopia. All of these ambassadors have wholeheartedly supported and encouraged the development of the OIC projects in their countries. We look forward to maintaining closer relationships with them and to developing meaningful relationships with ambassadors from all African countries from the Mediterranean to the Cape, from the Bulge to the Horn. We feel that not only is this our privilege, but also our responsibility.

The Power of the United and Praying Church

A SERMON

". . . I will build my church, and the powers of death shall not prevail against it."   *—Matthew 16:18*

A boy was walking through a field one day when he fell into a hole along the way. The hole was deep and dark. Unable to free himself from the hole he was in, the boy called out for help. "Someone come and help me!" he cried. A man passing by heard the cry of the boy. He walked to the edge of the hole and lowered a rope to the boy. The rope was not long enough, and so the man stood there listening to the cry of the boy. Another man passed by who heard the cry of the boy. He walked over to the edge of the hole. He too had a rope. He let his rope down, but it was not long enough. So the two men stood there with ropes in their hands listening to the cry of the boy. Another man passed by. He too had a rope in his hand. He walked over to the hole and let his rope down, but it, too, was not long enough. So the three men stood there by the edge of the hole listening to the cry of the boy, until at last the boy, looking up and seeing the three men standing there with ropes in their hands, cried out to them, "Put your ropes together and let them down to me." The three men tied their ropes together and let them down to the boy. And the boy took hold of the united ropes and pulled himself up to safety.

All around the world boys and girls and men and women are crying out for help. The sounds in our streets are cries for help from men and women, boys and girls who have fallen into a hole, deep and dark, by no fault of their own. They are not just the cries of Black men and women and boys and girls. The situation is far broader than that. The cries come from everywhere. Yes, from Watts, from Chicago, from Harlem, and from North Philadelphia; but also from the campuses of Columbia, Berkeley, Harvard, and Yale; from around the world, from Europe, from Asia, and from Africa; boys and girls and men and women are crying

148

out for help, characterized so clearly in the student crisis at the Sorbonne, several years ago, that nearly turned France upside down.

Yes, youth everywhere and adults, too, are caught in a hole crying out, striking out, struggling, fighting, rebelling, and wiggling without knowing quite what their struggle, their fighting, their rebellion, and their wiggling are all about. "Somebody!" they are crying out to us the best way they know how, "somebody come and help us!" The church must hear this cry, for the church is God's agency in this world. And the church must do more than react to it. The church must respond to it, for the church can play the greater part.

First, we must put the work of our churches together to reach and to lift our children to God. The concentration of our strength is becoming more and more the essential need of the church if we are to deal mightily and meaningfully with the problems before us. We must put our ropes together in united common effort, focusing on the problems of youth and prejudice and need in the streets and throughout the world in which men live. This calls for some revolutionary thinking and some revolutionary acting as far as the traditional church is concerned. It means giving up some things to gain some things. It means the church adapting herself to new circumstances, new challenges, and new missions. It means putting our ropes together, denominationally, as never before. Through centuries the church has been judged by its creeds, but today it is being judged by its deeds. People are not asking anymore what the church believes. The question now being asked is: "What is the church doing for the amelioration of the conditions of mankind?" The majority of people do not care about church doctrine. They are looking for a practical translation of the spirit of Jesus Christ in the everyday lives of people.

The church is sick with a fatal fever of inaction and detachment from the crucial problems of our day. While our buildings stand, our congregations fall apart. The church will never again draw and bind the masses to a communion by essays on faith, but by showing her faith by her works. As Oliver Wendell Holmes put it more than a half century ago,

> Away with your timeworn creeds
> Large professions and little deeds,

149

While freedom weeps
Wrong rules the land and
Waiting justice sleeps.

This cry is being echoed and reechoed in every town and hamlet in the civilized world. Christ came to give the world not a set of doctrines and creeds, but an example of manhood. He was manifested in the flesh to show us what God is and what man ought to be. Essays on faith are not enough now. Confessionals and creeds are not enough now. The deeds of a church are what count. There are men in perdition who can recite prayers, the Westminster Confession, the Apostles' Creed, and our other church covenants and articles of faith. There are men banished from God's presence who can discourse eloquently upon mysticism and dogmatism and higher criticism. No, it is not these abstractions that we need now for the masses, but men and churches and denominations who put their ropes together so that the boy in the pit at this crucial time can pull himself up to safety.

We must put our ropes together economically. A short time ago in the area of Philadelphia where I live, a church mortgaged itself and used the funds to assist the work in the concentrated community.[1] This is preaching at its best. Somehow the resources of the church must be focused upon the problems of the streets and the problems of the world as never before. We must mortgage ourselves to the cause of Christ, so that what we have may be extended to the growth of the spirit in mankind.

I believe that we have been unjustly critical of our children falling away from the church these days. If we would honestly analyze the emphasis of the church in the past and the present, we would find that it is to get men into heaven, rather than to get heaven into men; it is to keep men out of hell rather than to get hell out of men. In the minds of our young people, we have separated God from reality. If they seem not to follow our God, it is not because they do not believe in God or feel the need for him, for there is an ultimate reality in every man that longs for God. It is because they need *their* Savior, a Savior who speaks to *their* needs, a Savior who is relevant to *them* and *their times*. Jesus is that Savior, for Jesus speaks a message to the youth and to

[1] Richard L. Keach, *The Purple Pulpit* (Valley Forge: Judson Press, 1971).

the old as well. They need to know of a God who does not constantly say what they cannot do, but a God who says what they can do and how it can be done. "So send us a Savior," they cry, "a Savior that we can understand."

The hour has come for a concentrated action of all the religious forces and factors. The young people in every part of our world— of all races, colors, and climes—are waiting for a united effort on the part of all denominations for the salvation of the world. Youth is ready to join the march if they can see where we are going. This unity is developing more and more. Day by day we see illustrations of it—the merging of denominational groups, the fusing of worship services, and the joining of forces in Christian mission. Whether we like it or not, the huge hammer of the eternal gospel is destined to smash into smithereens the old sectarian shells which no longer have relevance to us and which have separated us and impeded the coming of the kingdom of heaven. The long hand of God's clock is silently but surely creeping toward the hour of the fulfillment of the prophecy and the prayer of Jesus when there shall be one shepherd and one fold. We must put our ropes together for a concerted attack on sin and God's foes.

Furthermore, we must put our ropes together in our attitudes, our thoughts, and our actions toward men who seem so strange to us and different from ourselves. If we want a Christian world, then let there be a Christian nation beginning with us. If we want Christian families, let us have a Christian family beginning with our own, in where we live, with no exceptions; in who lives with us, with no exceptions; with whom we work, with no exceptions; with whom we marry, with no exceptions. You ask over and over again, do you want your daughter to marry a man of another race? Yes, if she wants to, no exceptions. Put your ropes together and let them down to mean no exceptions.

The problem in our cities is the problem of our exceptions— housing exceptions, employment exceptions, social exceptions, and church exceptions. There must be no exceptions, for as long as there are exceptions there will be trouble in the streets and trouble in the nation and trouble in the world. "What do you want?" you ask. Everything you have, no exceptions. Not just equal—the same, no exceptions. This is what the cry is all about.

151

We must put our ropes together—no exceptions.

Finally, we must put our ropes together with our common prayers. For there is power in common prayer. We receive not because we ask not. We must put our ropes together in common prayer. Prayer is the medium through which we get power to live, to work, to accomplish what seems impossible. The world is in a spiritual and moral mess. Our cities and homes and churches are in a spiritual and moral mess, in many cases morally and spiritually bankrupt, powerless, because we no longer rely on the power and strength from on high. We no longer pray. Like a tree without sap, an automobile without a battery, there is nothing to move us on and nothing to make us go.

The apostle Paul said, "[He] is able to do exceeding abundantly above all that we ask or think, according to the power that worketh in us" (Ephesians 3:20, KJV). God has given us power, power to straighten out the world, the nations, the cities, the homes, ourselves, our youth, if we would pray. The need of the cities around the world is one of prayer. Jesus said, "All power is given unto me in heaven and earth," and if any of us haven't the power to do his will and his work, the trouble is not with Jesus, but with us. The mission of Jesus was to make the crooked way straight, the hilly way level, and the rough way smooth. Prayer changes things. Yes, there is power in the united and the praying church.

Be not forlorn. God has the answer. Put your ropes together and let them down to me.

Let us pray:

Eternal God, our heavenly Father, speak to our needs. Help us to know that thou art near to unite our thoughts and our actions toward the common purpose of the coming of the kingdom. Help us to pray that the day of the kingdom might come on earth as it is in heaven.

Amen.

Remarks at the Annual General Motors Stockholders' Meeting

May 21, 1971, Detroit, Michigan

Mr. Chairman and shareholders of the General Motors Corporation represented here:

I speak now on my own as a member of the Board of General Motors and as a stockholder. I do not own many General Motors shares, only five, but for a Baptist preacher, that is pretty good. It is my intention to do better.

I accepted membership on the General Motors Board with mixed feelings. I am basically a man who identifies with the plight, the needs, and the aspirations of the ordinary man, and particularly the Black man. I really did not know how I would fare in this new role as a member of the General Motors Board, because I am an outspoken person, unwilling to permit my voice or my opinions to be controlled by anyone.

I came to General Motors Board wanting to help General Motors to build and to grow and to make profits and to progress. Yet, in so doing, I have also wanted to help the development and the growth and the progress of the minority population of the nation, Black, Chicano, Puerto Rican, Oriental, and others who strive for full recognition and economic opportunity in America.

I am glad to report that I have been encouraged by my reception from my fellow board members these past months. Already I am seeing some good things happen that make me believe the company is headed in the right direction, especially as far as opportunities for minorities are concerned.

You can be sure that you will be hearing more of my assessment about progress in these areas as time goes on. We have a long, long, long way to go in upgrading job opportunities and making available opportunities in middle-management, supervisory, and corporate jobs for Blacks and Americans of color for promotions and opportunities in sales and dealerships and in other categories.

I should like to say I, too, would like to see more definitive recording and reporting of our progress in these areas. But at this particular time, I am encouraged. We shall see in the future, regarding these things, what we shall see.

My reason for speaking today, though, regards the General Motors involvement in the Union of South Africa. Apartheid is the most ruthless and dehumanizing practice perpetuated in the world today. Blacks in the Union of South Africa are relegated to subhuman treatment without freedom of movement, without economic equality in wages for the same job performed and without even basic elemental rights. Apartheid must come to an end.

To a great measure the system of apartheid is being underwritten by American industry, interests, and investments, simply by virtue of our operations there. There are over three hundred American businesses and companies operating in the Union of South Africa today, including the General Motors Corporation. These companies by their very presence are helping to sustain the existence of this terrible practice I have alluded to today. Either the leaders of the Union of South Africa will end apartheid in the Union of South Africa or one day apartheid will mean the end of the Union of South Africa—and everything General Motors has in it.

But, even more than economic considerations or political considerations, American industry cannot morally continue to do business in a country that so blatantly and ruthlessly and clearly maintains such dehumanizing practices against such large numbers of its people.

Admittedly, my concern goes even deeper. When I realize I am a Black man and that the vast majority of those who are dehumanized are Black like myself, I hear voices say to me: "Things will work out in time, things are getting better, let us slow down on this matter." But then I ask, *"Why does the world always want to go slow when the rights of Black men are at stake?"*

In America, in South Africa, in any place in the world where this situation is known, I am vocally supporting the position of the Executive Council of the Protestant Episcopal Church in this matter.

I want to go on record for all to know that I will continue to pursue my desire to see that American enterprises, including General Motors, withdraw from the Union of South Africa until clear changes have been made in the practices and the policies of that government as they pertain to the treatment of Blacks and other nonwhites. I have no desire to be spectacular. I want to see GM out of the contemporary unparalleled oppressive situation that exists there.

I have no desire but to help this company. I say to you, if you help the world in this matter, the world will help General Motors. So, I advocate a vote for proposal VIII, as I have taken that position on the board. And although I know I shall lose today, I shall continue to pursue this interest tomorrow, until Black people in the Union of South Africa are free.

Testimony Before Congressional Subcommittee on Africa Concerning Position Against Apartheid

Mr. Chairman (Congressman Diggs), distinguished members of this committee, I am honored to have this opportunity to express my views before this subcommittee on Africa.

Apartheid must come to an end. There is a tide sweeping across the world, and that tide is sweeping in the direction of freedom and liberty and opportunity, and not in the direction of segregation, discrimination, or apartheid. Apartheid is the most inhuman practice against people we know of in the world today. Apartheid means division of all kinds—physical, economic, political, psychological, and religious. This system has to be ended, and I want to see America take the lead in the world in ending it. This can primarily be done, as I see it, by economic means.

Being a Baptist preacher, I know that to save a soul you take away the sin. To rid the world of apartheid, you take away its profits. To hit apartheid where it hurts, you must hit it in the pocketbook. There are three hundred American-based businesses involved directly and indirectly in the Union of South Africa. One-third of the productivity in the Union of South Africa can be traced in some part, large or small, to American business investment and development and production on either a large or a small scale.

I think it would be well to acknowledge at this point that I not only come before this committee to voice my opinion, and that of the Opportunities Industrialization Centers with programs in one hundred cities across America as well as Nigeria, Ghana, and developing in other parts of Africa, but I am here expressing the consensus of much of the American public, and I might add, the unanimous convictions, to my knowledge, of our African American population.

Also, before I begin to state more fully my views concerning South Africa and the American practice and policy toward this section of the African continent, all of us here today must understand very clearly that we Americans of African descent are determined to play a major role in shaping, influencing, and developing a more effective and positive new United States policy toward South Africa and the Black continent of Africa, a policy that will be mutually and equally beneficial to both countries.

I am sure we are all aware of the growing expression on the part of Black America as it relates to America's international policies, more particularly its policy toward South Africa, as well as the total dark continent. With this increasing identification I am here today and I will be back tomorrow, and the day after, to make certain that our views are heard and that one day they will be implemented as best they can be implemented, considering all factors that will prevail.

In discussing South Africa and the South African situation, I should also state that my concerns are not just emotional ones. Even though we are truly and deeply emotional over what is happening in this unhappy part of Africa, we are equally concerned from a pragmatic and a very realistic, democratic point of view raised in this country. We, as Black Americans and Americans generally, have been taught all our lives, and even now, that democracy is the best form of government and it is based on the concept of majority rule guaranteeing the interest and development of the minorities.

We have been taught that democracy is based upon a representative government, the concept and practice that citizens through the right to vote (one man—one vote) would voice their

156

concern informing the institutions and personalities that govern. In other words, we were taught that a democratic society looks equally after the well-being and pursuit of happiness of all its peoples. May I add we have been taught that these principles were universal truths that not only apply to America, but also must one day apply throughout the world embracing all mankind.

Now I am certain that all you gentlemen here today would agree with this general and brief description of democracy as stated above. If this is so, why is it necessary for us, 195 years after independence, to be sitting here debating what form of polices we shall have toward the undemocratic regime of South Africa that is the antithesis of everything that democracy in America stands for? What we should be doing at this point in history is implementing ideas to assist the people of South Africa toward their liberation, their political and economic freedom.

We don't mean necessarily through dialogue, as seems so popular in our many quarters. What we should be implementing here today is the creation of active assistance by our nation to free not only South Africa, but Rhodesia, Angola, and Mozambique. We may look at our simple but basic description of what democracy is on one hand, and compare it with what is at work in South Africa. We can see without a doubt, that nothing resembling democracy and justice exists in this section of Africa, the continent that is the origin of thirty million African Americans like myself.

The racial discrimination practiced pervades every aspect of South African life. Out of a total population of nineteen million people, there are four Blacks to every one nonblack, yet the Blacks have no say or direct involvement in government. The governing White Supremacy National Party has made it a clear determination to pursue a policy of apartheid. The Africans, who play a major role in the country's labor force providing nearly all farm labor, 90 percent of mine workers, 75 percent of the manufacturing force, and a major portion of public service employees, are barred from not only governing their own country but also from even participating in any way except as slave laborers.

Presently the so-called government of South Africa is attempting to realize its policy of apartheid by forcibly restricting 68 percent of the South African population to 14 percent of the land, and the land of nineteen million people is totally controlled and governed in a Fascist dictatorial manner by a small alien minority of three million. Can you call this even the semblance of the beginning of the democracy we espouse and hope to preach around the world at all, much less at its best?

If this is what you call democracy and this is what the United States government and industry can stand for and support, if this is what we want to see continue, then we as believers in democracy, we as American citizens, we as Black Americans, proud of our African heritage, must state here loud and clear that we cannot, and will not, tolerate this policy of supporting and encouraging this minority rule over a majority who are our brothers from our land of heritage. We cannot in all honesty be committed to the basic principles of democracy and still support continuing American involvement, whether it be government or private enterprise, in this undemocratic situation in South Africa.

Now, many people say that if the United States government and businesses would pull out, this would hurt the African people on that part of the continent. Well, let me speak to that voice. My brothers and sisters in Africa say that they disagree with this utterance. These are just the voices of those who want to continue doing business as usual, maintaining the status quo. If you say we should be thin-skinned and support doing business as usual, because a few men and women have jobs out of the ordinary, it is like supporting a Black man with a job making hot dogs at a segregated lunch counter.

We know that the only successful way in bringing about the downfall of the undemocratic regime of South Africa is to weaken its economic foundation, to hit apartheid where it hurts most, to hit it in the pocketbook. We know from experience that a man cannot live by bread alone. We know that spiritual food, food of dignity, is just as important as those essentials provided by economic activity.

We, like our African brothers, are willing to suffer by having the United States and other Western countries impose a complete and total embargo against South Africa. We know that our brothers can suffer no more than they are suffering now.

Today you hear many people talking about a dialogue with the minority government. You hear many people talk about a dialogue with the minority government of South Africa. We believe in dialogue, too, if it is a dialogue of silence toward White minority government rule. We believe in dialogue as the American people tell their government to sever all its relationships with this dictatorial minority-ruled government. We believe in dialogue if it means the shareholders of the big United States corporate investors in South Africa telling their boards of directors that they must cease any economic transactions with this repressive government.

Yes, let's have a dialogue, but let it be a dialogue in the spirit of America and the dialogue of democracy—the dialogue of one man, one vote. If the present South African government wants to continue relations or have a dialogue with America, governmental and political, and if the South African government wants to keep American industries in their nation, in my opinion and view they must accomplish the following with all considerable dispatch:

1. Do away with the need for Blacks carrying identification cards.

2. Take down all the restricted Black Only, White Only, Colored Only, signs throughout the country, and get rid of policies of separation.

3. Grant freedom of movement for African peoples throughout the country of South Africa.

4. Grant the African people equal wages for equal work.

5. Grant the Black population the right to vote and to hold government positions.

These are the five elemental requests. They can be done almost overnight, for all you need to do to remove the signs is to use a screwdriver. But until this is done, I recommend to this distinguished committee the following course of action for a needed implementation:

First, that the United States government support the U.N. in the pronouncement it has already made on this matter, also the Organization of African Unity resolution of economic and military embargo of South Africa; and that the United States should encourage its allies to do likewise, especially Britain, Germany, France, and Japan.

Second, that the United States government break all diplomatic relations with South Africa, *all of it;* withdraw its ambassadors and official representatives, and insist that American industry follow suit.

Third, that the United States withdraw all its economic and political dealings with the Portuguese government, which is suppressing the liberation and aspiration of the people of Angola and Mozambique.

Fourth, that the United States government, working through the Organization of African Unity (OAU) and bilateral agreement with African countries, provide more financial and technical assistance to help bring equality and opportunity and education for the Black and colored peoples in southern Africa.

Fifth, that all American-based industries and businesses pull out of the Union of South Africa until apartheid is ended.

Sixth, that the United States government and private industry assist the remainder of the continent in speeding up its economic and social development by extending larger and more generous provisions of aid and investments principally in Black Africa; and that the United States government and private enterprises begin to support and encourage larger African-American involvement on the African continent.

We believe that these steps are needed to change the situation in Africa: in southern Africa and in all of Africa. Also, we feel that these efforts, in the long run, will be to the advantage of America and to the whole world as we strive for universal peace. I want to see, Mr. Chairman, the American flag fly for liberty around the world again. I want my Black brothers and sisters in South Africa to be free. I am aware that in speaking as I do, I lose strong friends who perhaps will not support my work in the future, but I cannot keep quiet in a day like this if I believe in my destiny and if I have faith in the potential of the Black man. My conscience will not permit me to be silent whatever my loss might be and the loss of my programs, for God will take care of me.

Again, I thank all of you for having this opportunity to address this important hearing.

I have spoken what I have spoken. Perhaps I can start a ripple that will make a wave that will make a tide that will make a change for my brothers in southern Africa.

DATE DUE

AP 1 9'83			
GAYLORD			PRINTED IN U.S.A